THE
LANGDALES

THE LANGDALES

LANDSCAPE AND PREHISTORY IN A LAKELAND VALLEY

MARK EDMONDS

TEMPUS

For Dagmar

First published 2004

Tempus Publishing Ltd
The Mill, Brimscombe Port
Stroud, Gloucestershire GL5 2QG
www.tempus-publishing.com

© Mark Edmonds, 2004

The right of Mark Edmonds to be identified as the Author
of this work has been asserted by him in accordance with the
Copyrights, Designs and Patents Act 1988.

All rights reserved. No part of this book may be reprinted
or reproduced or utilised in any form or by any electronic,
mechanical or other means, now known or hereafter invented,
including photocopying and recording, or in any information
storage or retrieval system, without the permission in writing
from the Publishers.

British Library Cataloguing in Publication Data.
A catalogue record for this book is available from the British Library.

ISBN 0 7524 3238 9

Typesetting and origination by Tempus Publishing.
Printed and bound in Great Britain.

CONTENTS

	PREFACE	7
CHAPTER 1	BEYOND THE FRAME	11
CHAPTER 2	AN EXTENSION OF THE HAND	33
CHAPTER 3	WOODWORK	47
CHAPTER 4	POETRY IN AN UNKNOWN LANGUAGE	67
CHAPTER 5	TENURE	97
CHAPTER 6	STONEWORK	127
CHAPTER 7	TRUTH TO MATERIAL	153
CHAPTER 8	OVERLAPPING WORLDS	171
CHAPTER 9	ENDINGS	191
	NOTES	203
	BIBLIOGRAPHY	215
	INDEX	221

PREFACE

This is not going to be a book about the Lakes, but about the ways people look at the Lakes; not about the fells but about a view of the fells . . .

With these words the poet Norman Nicholson opened his book *The Lakers*, the title taken from a satirical play published by James Plumtre in 1798. In what followed, he laid out the historical and social geography of tourism in the Lake District, an affectionate yet critical account of the making of an English Arcadia – the accounts of the first 'explorers' and the vision of the early guides; the caricatures of the Picturesque and the closer focus of the Romantics. Taking the area through to the moral landscapes of John Ruskin at the back end of the nineteenth century, he charted how the place opened up to different audiences, each with their own particular visions.

Nicholson was passionate about the area and its history. He returned again and again to the close relationship between people and land. Not land as an abstracted symbol or artistic subject, but as terrain and materials that influenced identity. What comes through is his frustration that the tourist gaze saw only part of this picture, and even that through a tinted glass. When I first started walking in the Lakes in my teens, I had little idea about the history of this aesthetic. Despite the best efforts of several teachers, the writings and paintings of the Romantics had failed to strike a major chord. I was taken by the Langdales even then, but didn't know how the area had come to be regarded at the time, still less how that had influenced my choice, like many others, for one of the first holidays I had taken on my own. I didn't know where the 'outward bound' mentality came from.

The Langdales

To be honest, I'm not sure that I recognised just how much the responses documented by Nicholson influenced my thinking when I came back to work in the area in the late 1980s, still less how they underpinned much of what we now call 'landscape archaeology'. Since then, I have had to change my views. There have been many times when I found myself back on the same crags, sometimes as part of a group, sometimes on my own, and each return has strengthened a sense that there was much that I had missed; about my connection with the area, and how things might have been in the past. Part of the problem was a failure to connect the process of history with the lived experiences of people. Most of all, I began to recognise that between the Romantic tradition and the Neolithic, there was a long and complex history of lives played out across the area which I had not really thought about. The 'way of seeing' fostered over the last few centuries made it difficult to see very different connections. It is this, perhaps more than anything else, that has brought me back to writing about the Langdales.

The return has also been a challenge in another way. Most guides to the area make at least some gesture towards the work that went on above the heads of what has since become a valley community. Some encourage prospection; even Wainwright has a drawing of a roughout. This has bought its own crop of problems, including illicit digging and the casual appropriation of worked stone found along the path. This is a major concern; the sites are very vulnerable, prone to erosion and easily damaged, the threat all the more serious because they are so rare. Even when people pick up stone with the best of intentions and take it to a museum there are problems, because we learn as much from the context of the find as from the stone itself. The conservation issues raised are a nightmare and that is why I have not provided a sharply detailed map of sites across the area. What follows has been written in the hope that a sketch of just what it is that makes this place so remarkable will encourage all of us to tread more carefully.

CHAPTER 1

BEYOND THE FRAME

The Stake exhibits a miniature of very bad Alpine road, across a mountain, not just perpendicular, and about five miles over. The road makes many traverses so close, that at every flexure it seems almost to return into itself. In descending the Stake, on the Langdale side, a cataract accompanies you on the left, with all the horrors of a precipice. Langdale Pike, called Pike a Stickle and Steel Pike is an inaccessible pyramidal rock and commands the whole. Here nature seems to have discharged all her useless load of matter and rock, when form was first impressed on chaos . . .
        (Thomas West, *A Guide to the Lakes*, 1778)

AN EYE TO PERCEIVE

The Langdales have long been favoured by painters. For well over two centuries, people like Gainsborough and Hills, Turner, Constable and many others have visited the area, creating a rich legacy of images. Fanciful panoramas and intense religious treatments, bruised watercolours and sketches with an almost scientific attention to detail. Among many views, the skyline that balances Harrison, Loft Crag and the dome of the more distant Pike of Stickle has proved especially popular. Easels set up near Skelwith Force, cars pausing on the road by Harry Place to snap from the window. Made all the more familiar through reproduction, this view from the south-east appears in

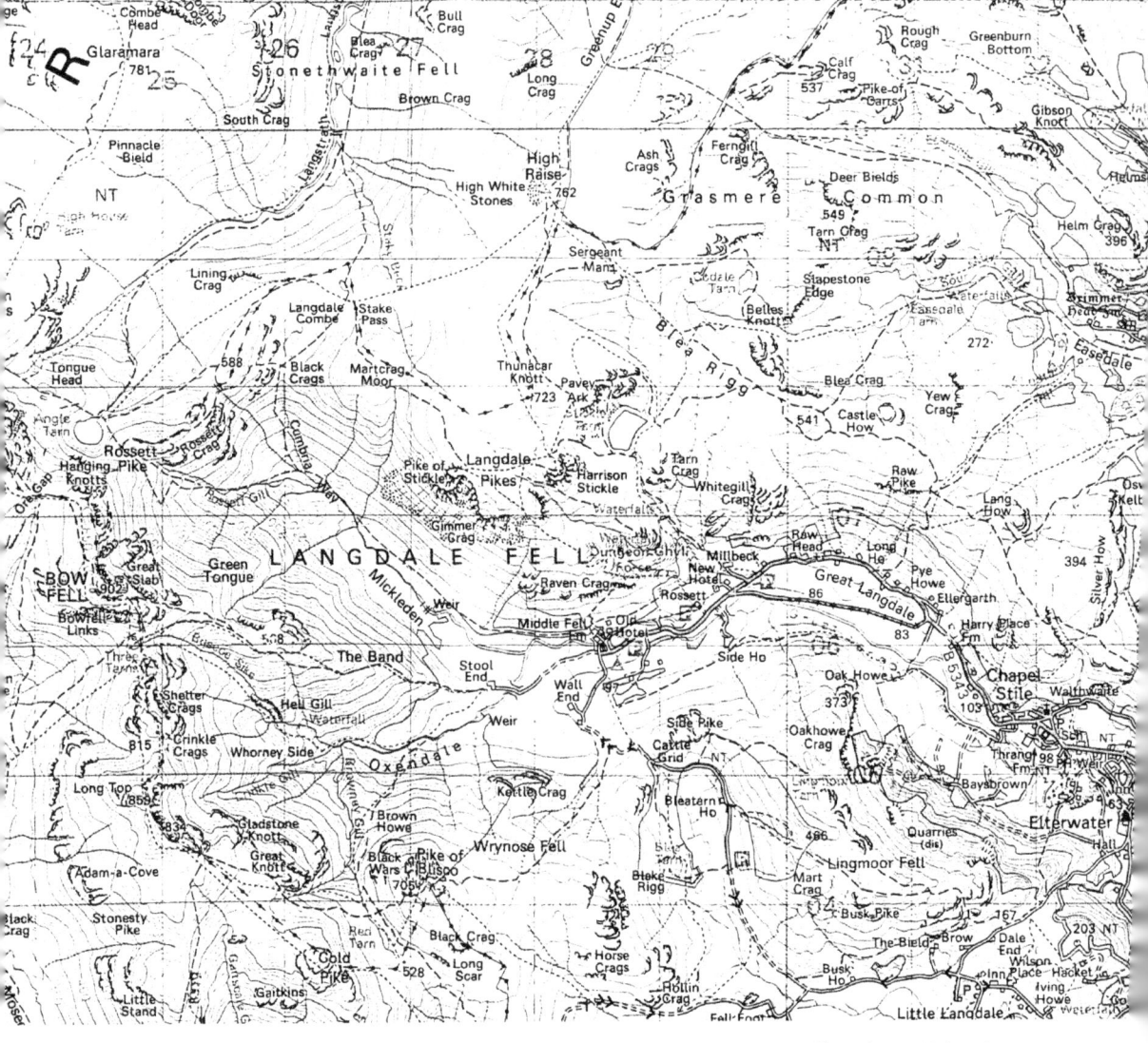

Reproduced from Ordnance Survey mapping on behalf of The Controller of Her Majesty's Stationery Office © Crown Copyright 100042822 2004

prints, on postcards and on boxes of fudge; repeated so often it has become generic – somewhere and nowhere in particular. The 'lusty twins' of Wordsworth's *Excursion* brooding in the background, the cleft of Dungeon Ghyl bringing the eye down, water often spilling to meet you near the bottom of the frame. My grandmother in South London had the same scene on a biscuit tin, though I didn't recognise it at the time. That may be why the area seemed strangely familiar on my first visit.

This is not a book about painting. It is a sketch of some of the ways in which the Langdales have been lived in and perceived over time, ways of relating to land and to others that have left their mark on dale and fell. In particular, it is a journey into the Neolithic, when scattered groups travelled to the crags to make axes from a distinctive grey-green stone. It is an attempt to imagine the world in which this work was important and what this meant at the time. This is not an easy journey to make. The evidence is fragmented, the path far from clear; in the words of William Gilpin, much is 'wrapped in obscurity'. As if that was not enough, the going is made even harder because our perception of the area today is the legacy of painters and poets. Much of our way of seeing and of thinking is the product of a projection no more than a few centuries old.

The frame for this projection was established in the eighteenth century, when the 'Lake District' was carved out of Cumberland, Westmorland and Lancashire-north-of-the-sands. What had long been regarded by many outsiders as rough and uninviting country was shifted from the margins and became the subject of an aesthetic – 'The Picturesque'.[1] This way of seeing had very particular roots. It emerged at a time when enclosure and improvement were transforming many parts of the country, when the control of large estates lay squarely in the hands of the gentry and the aristocracy. A time when towns were rapidly expanding, urban populations swelled by those who had lost their tenure and their living in the country. More specifically, it grew out of arguments about nature and landscape amongst an educated and landed elite, those who felt their fingers were on the pulse of cultural debate. It became a subject on the lips of all who considered themselves a part of 'Polite Society'.

During the second half of the eighteenth century, the English Arcadia drew the polite classes in droves, many with 'Claude glasses' to frame and tint the view, some with sketch books and paints.[2] Primed by Burke's *Enquiry into the Beautiful and the Sublime*, by West's *Guide to the Lakes* and by Gilpin's *Observations*, they moved between designated 'stations' on a secular pilgrimage to the Picturesque. They came because it was fashionable to do so, an equivalent for the Grand Tour of Europe that did not require the crossing of volatile national boundaries. They toured and sketched because the area seemed to offer a reassuring contrast to the realities of life at the time. And they marvelled at the scenery because by then, primed by those early guides and essays, the

Robert Hills. *Skelwith Force*. Birmingham City Museum and Art Gallery

'Lake District' had emerged as an area of national importance, an icon of stability and harmony.

The Lakes had all that was needed for the making of 'classic ground' outside the flow of modern life. Here were the ingredients of a changeless classical paradise located squarely within the boundaries of the nation.[3] Gently rolling pastures and beautiful water, a mix of open ground and sylvan shadow, sublime and sometimes terrifying mountains that could stand in for the Alps. There were even fragments from antiquity, equivalents for the shattered temples and broken statuary that littered the Arcadian scenes of Salvator, Claude and Poussin. Ruined abbeys and places like the 'Druidical Circle' at Castlerigg, documented by West and Hutchinson and painted by Pyne and many others. Those with the capital went even further, augmenting their scenes at a one to one scale. Around Windermere in particular, the late eighteenth and early nineteenth centuries saw the construction of elaborate, often classically inspired villas on lakesides and islands. These were valued parts of the prospect, in keeping with the aesthetic sensibilities of the time.[4] And like the halls and parks where nature was no less tailored to a certain point of view, they were also exclusive. Places where those of the right sort could meet to admire the scenery, hold parties and regattas, even fire cannons on the lake to catch the echoes as they rolled back off the fells.[5] Though they were often no more than a backdrop to the water, the fells were an essential element in this scene. An expression of the Sublime, the skyline of the Langdales balanced many conventional views of Windermere or Skelwith Force, the crags sometimes exaggerated to suit the tastes of the day.

Conventions were by no means fixed. After the wanderings of the first 'explorers' and the influence of early guides, many poets, painters and commentators became critical of popular panoramas and the manipulation of landscapes to make pleasing scenes.[6] Particularly vocal were the Romantics, who struggled to look closer, not just at the land or at fragments of antiquity, but at the more basic relation of humanity to nature. Their views in turn were adapted by others, among them John Ruskin, and as the nineteenth century progressed, Arcadia gradually opened up to different audiences; the gentry, the urban middle classes and finally, those who worked beneath the ground or in factories spread across the Midlands and the North. And yet for all of the argument back and forth, there was one feature – or lack of it – that many images of the area shared throughout much of this time. People are rare in most views; absent altogether or present only in particular and idealised forms.

In some prints it is the gentry themselves who feature, usually in the foreground and on or near the border of the image – sometimes in their finery, sometimes in costumes with a classical twist. Like those who visited galleries or purchased pictures for their drawing rooms, they are as much observers of the scene as they are part of it. In other pictures, figures take a different position. From the early stages of the Picturesque, there is often a shepherd or two in the foreground or the middle field, their dress, like the ruins nearby, tending towards the classical. Such images would have been familiar if you kept up with the literature, with Virgilian Georgic and then Pastoral poetry. Even those who tried to move beyond an evocation of Arcadia tend to repeat this idealised form. Accompanied by lines from *Paradise Lost* when exhibited at the Royal Academy in 1798, Turner's powerful rendering of the Langdales places a couple and their sheep where the foreground meets the fells. The figures, like so many, are sketchy. But there is enough to evoke a sense of the first couple in the time before 'The Fall'.

The couple in Turner's scene have many counterparts. The figures in most eighteenth- and early nineteenth-century prints of the Lakes are usually small in size and number; sketched in bucolic poses which suggest quiet contemplation rather than graft. They seem to be part of the land, engaged in activities as stable and timeless as the lakes and fells themselves, as if they were living in some form of changeless 'natural' state. That may be why their gaze seldom connects directly with the viewer in the way that was common in portraits of the gentry themselves. They were part of the scenery; the gentry owned it.

These idealised and increasingly sentimental treatments extend out to buildings and to the broader landscape. Signs of people's relationship with the land are few and far between and when they do appear, they once again take a stylised form. Cottages are almost always isolated and small scale; architecture and life around romanticised and calm. As Thomas Gray put it in the late 1760s '. . . all is peace, rusticity, and happy poverty, in its neatest and most becoming attire . . .'; always that way, always there. There are few signs of mining villages, of improvement or the broader forces changing the landscapes of the time. There is certainly little sign of unrest or of poverty that was less than 'happy'. Walls become antiquated or disappear altogether and only rarely do quarrying or other industries get a look in, usually in sketches rather than larger canvases. Much the same treatment can be found in many of the journals, guides and articles written by and for a polite audience. Tales of eccentric and largely innocent folk who seemed to exist outside the flow of normal time, isolated from modernity by the barrier of the mountains. People like the 'Maid of Buttermere' or 'The Solitary' of Blea Tarn House – people without history.

These images are revealing. Coleridge could write in dramatic and hallucinatory detail about the form of 'mad water' as it twisted and turned down a fall. Artists could spend hours composing scenes, catching changes in the surface of a lake and shifts of light across the fells. But the requirement to look closely extended only rarely to those who actually lived in the area. Indeed, the more common observation was that the natives might be spoilt by the cash that tourism brought with it, an opinion repeated more recently on a global scale. Even Wordsworth raised an eyebrow at the caricature. In an early pastoral, *The Brothers*, he contrasts those who work the land with dilettante sketchers, who: '. . . Upon the forehead of a jutting crag. Sit perch'd with

Seen the other way: from the head of Great Langdale, looking back towards the top of Windermere.
Photo: Bob Bewley

book and/ pencil on their knee,/ And look and scribble, scribble on and look,/ Until a man might travel twelve stout miles,/ Or reap an acre of his neighbour's corn'.

Wordsworth does not cultivate the open field sensibilities of poets like John Clare. The radical vision which had carried him to revolutionary France in his youth was replaced by a more nostalgic and conservative view when he gazed upon landscapes closer to home. He often romanticises the pastoral covenant of agrarian life, paying less attention to those around him than his sister Dorothy. But his work nonetheless finds a tension between simply looking at a landscape and living in it. In another poem, *Michael*, he strengthens the contrast, fastening with an archaeological fascination upon 'a straggling heap of unhewn stones'. All that remains of an unfinished sheepfold, the rubble becomes the touchstone for a lament to an independent farming family who lose their son to the city and fall upon hard times. Here and throughout *The Prelude*, the excavation of his memory uncovers a more intimate relationship between people, land and history – a sense of a stable, almost righteous inhabitation that he could not find in London or on the improved prairie of

Exaggerated crags loomed large in the literature too. Under the pseudonym of 'Rambler', Captain Joseph Budworth described a climb of the Pike of Stickle that he made for the sake of 'curiousity' in 1792. Led by a local farmer, Paul Postlethwaite, he was so overcome by the drop that he could only descend wearing blinkers, unable to contemplate '. . . the vast precipice almost perpendicularly under me . . .' Local accounts from the time suggest that Paul Postlethwaite saw things rather differently. Familiar with the terrain, he reserved a sense of awe for the size of the Captain's appetite. Mill Beck, Great Langdale. Thomas Allom 1835. Kendal Library

Blea Tarn House. Photo: Geoffrey Berry

Salisbury Plain. A fading connection missed by those who breezed in and out, going for the quick sensation and the required view.

That required view was from a very definite perspective. The idealised image of nature and the rural was something around which those of the 'right sort' combined. Part fabrication, part oversight, it painted over the consequences of enclosure, industry and improvement. And it did so most often for the very people introducing changes on their estates that cut across traditional and customary forms of living, changes that provoked resistance and unrest. The image of a stable and contented rural tradition was not just a refuge from the city; it was also something to hide behind.[7] It served other interests too. When Wordsworth claimed the Lake District as 'a sort of national property', he was claiming it for members of a particular class, those with 'an eye to perceive and a heart to enjoy'. But he was able to make such a claim because that romanticised image of an unchanged rural landscape was by then an established part of the origin myth of the nation, an implication of deep roots. Poverty, unrest and a strong regional tradition of non-conformity only confused the picture.

The Langdales

COASTAL EROSION

This image has proved remarkably persistent. Packaged now as landscape heritage, it stares out from tourist brochures and from gift shop windows in Ambleside, Keswick and Bowness. And though it finds a different audience to the one that Wordsworth might have imagined or desired, people are still a minor element in many scenes, history little more than timelessness. The Romantic legacy is such that it is hard to look at Cumbria without seeing 'The Lakes', hard to talk about history across the region without falling back upon the stereotype. It is, of course, a fiction. Outside the frame, life has seldom been that small scale, nor has it been constant – only perhaps in the world of Beatrix Potter. Even the hill farmers lamented in *The Prelude* were a part of broader worlds, their ways of living and of seeing specific to the politics of their time.

Things become more fluid the further back you go; the name and even the location of the region far from constant. Cumbria is in the mid-west of Britain

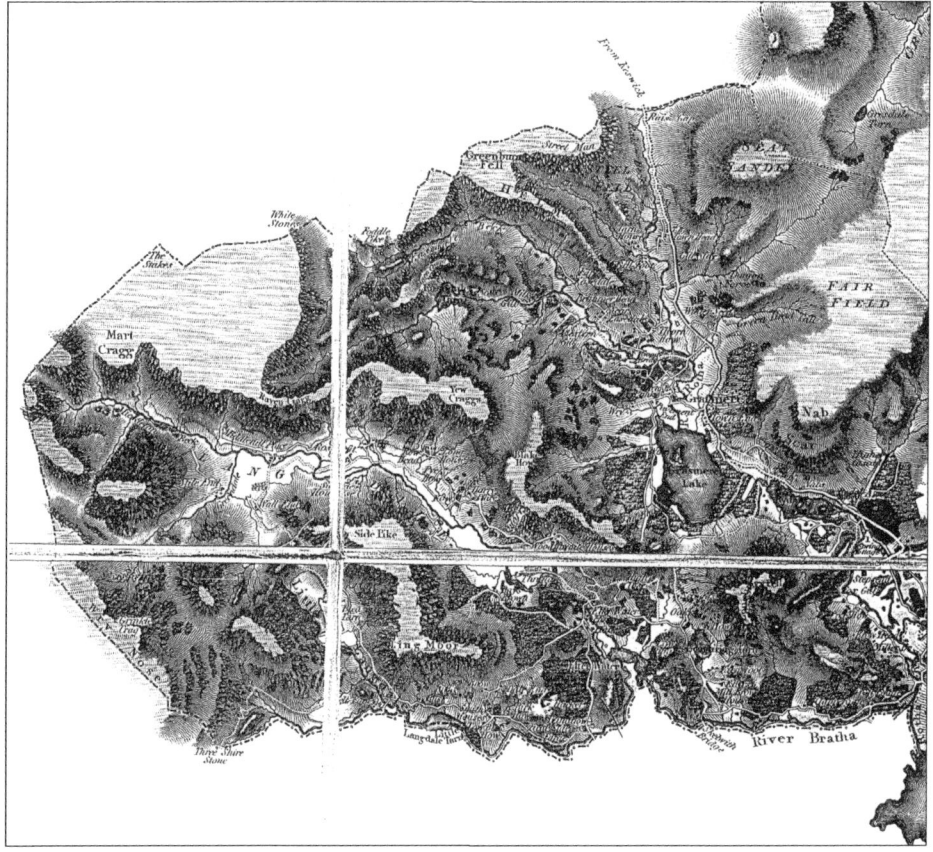

Exercising the engraver's art. The Great Langdale valley, with Little Langdale at the southern edge, seen here in Greenwood's map of 1824. Kendal Record Office

but the north-west of England and that distinction has often mattered. During the Roman occupation, it was important for a time as an area that could supply the forts and garrisons of the north, sometimes holding border status. From the fifth century onwards, it faced north and west, a reflection of more routine contact between clan-based 'kingdoms' around the margins of the Irish Sea. The boundaries of these regimes were by no means fixed. Much of northern Cumbria formed part of the Kingdom of Rheged, which extended into southern Scotland, but these were volatile times and by the seventh century, the area was recognised as part of the Anglian kingdom of Northumbria. By the tenth century, it had seen a significant influx of people from Scotland, Ireland and Scandinavia and parts of it were formally under Scottish dynastic control soon afterwards. It was only in the decades after the Norman Conquest that it emerged as the far flung north-western corner of England and even this was locally contested at the time. Names and allegiances have shifted at different scales ever since.[8]

When the focus shifts back more than five thousand years to the Neolithic, there is relatively little we can take as given. There's the shape of the land of course; the central fells and dales, the undulating forelands, the valleys and the coast. We can assume that these set at least some potentials for patterns of living and moving. But that is probably about it. What different areas looked like, how they were lived in and thought about, bore little relation to the taken-for-granted's that we've fostered since the eighteenth century. Even the most basic boundaries are far from secure; the edges like a rag torn from a larger cloth. In Langdale, two centuries of paintings, prints and poetry have brought the frame in close, the farms hunkered down on the lower slopes rendered as permanent fixtures. In the Neolithic, things were otherwise:

> We can hardly escape the conclusion that our great circles were built by seafaring people, coming from the south, who saw black combe from the sea and settled round its foot, later working their way up the coast and inland along the great valleys . . . They must have lived in the forest, and therefore they must have known how to make clearings and cultivate them, living perhaps in wigwam villages and moving on, like many forest tribes today, to clear a new patch when the soil of one was exhausted, but never going far from their circle which was the religious centre of the tribe. Some tribes may have had wooden circles instead, and these may yet be discovered, by searching Low Furness with an aeroplane. But none of them could live without cutting down trees; and we know how they did that: with stone axes. . .

So said R.G. Collingwood in his address to the 'Cumberland and Westmorland Antiquarian and Archaeological Society' in Appleby in 1932. He was talking about the Neolithic and the routes by which he imagined that colonists entered the region from the sea at that time. Collingwood was writing at a peculiar moment in the history of archaeology. Earlier generations of scholars had split their attentions between crude theories of social evolution and the painstaking documentation of the antiquities that had first fascinated the aristocracy and the gentry. By the early decades of the twentieth century and particularly after the First World War, the focus had shifted. Description and discovery were still important, in fact never more so. But many archaeologists had shaken off the grander narrative in favour of what we now call 'Culture History'. Broader arguments and comparisons were also still important, but these were received through the filter of an approach that looked for the particular histories of cultural groups; their appearance, movement and persistence across a Europe that was divided along strong national and ethnic lines.

For many scholars of Collingwood's era, what was important about the Neolithic was that it was a period when several things seemed to change at once. People started using pottery and polishing stone tools such as axes. They took on domesticated plants and animals and they even built monuments, tombs and enclosures. For him, this appeared to herald the beginning of a way of life and an attitude towards nature more familiar than that found in the earlier phases of the Stone Age. And the most likely explanation for these changes at the time was the influx of new people and ideas, a process of migration or diffusion from other regions which could be traced in a new way of living, in the styles of artefacts and in monumental architectures. Collingwood's paper remains one of the more considered and locally specific pieces of writing about the prehistory of what we now call Cumbria. He knows his way around the geography of the three counties as well as the archaeology. The address, like his other work, also reflects a sharp and original grasp of just how challenging it is to make sense of these fragments from our vantage in a very different world.[9] Things are no less challenging today.

One advantage that we do have is our ability to draw upon material unavailable in Collingwood's time. For example, scatters of Mesolithic flintwork, pollen cores and other evidence have all shown that people were a significant presence in the region long before the Neolithic. Groups who followed migrating game over massive distances soon after the retreat of the ice; hunters and gatherers who turned in smaller circles as tundra gave way to richer and more varied conditions. We also know that many of the things Collingwood attributed to the Neolithic did not arrive in a tight package 'off the boat'; life was not suddenly transformed by a wave of colonists. In fact, there was much continuity across the line we draw between the two periods. Many pollen profiles show few signs of change[10] and it is likely that artefacts such as microliths, which are usually attributed to the Mesolithic, were still being made in the early fourth millennium when Neolithic stone axes and pottery start to appear.[11] It is also likely that most of the stone circles in the area are later in date, some of the smaller circles not established until the Early Bronze Age.[12]

Merzbarn. The area has continued to draw powerful responses from artists. One of the more original of these was Kurt Schwitters, who worked in Langdale in the late 1940s to produce his third 'Merzbau' wall in a barn known locally as 'Cylinders' that had once served as a powder house for the Elterwater Gunpowder Company. Incorporating materials retrieved from farms, quarries and other detritus, the mural took up the end wall of the barn. Schwitters died in 1948, but the mural remained in place until 1965 when it (and the wall) was removed in one piece for transport to Newcastle University. Hatton Gallery, Bridgeman Art Gallery. Copyright DACS

Another of the key advantages that we have over Collingwood is that we have more time. He was writing before the development of radiocarbon (C14) dating, and relied upon comparative methods to establish chronologies. These were systematic and often reliable in relative terms. But they significantly underestimated the absolute dates and duration of the sequence. The developments he attributed to the arrival of specific cultural groups actually unfolded over more than three thousand years, the Neolithic just a part of that, spanning the period from *c*.4000–2000 BC. Just as the pollen blurs the boundary between the Mesolithic and the Neolithic[13], so this extension undermines the idea that the Neolithic disembarked fully formed when a flotilla made landfall below Black Combe. Things changed. But they did so in a protracted and piecemeal fashion, varying in timing and character from one part of the region to another.[14] Some people may well have moved into the area around the start of what we call the Neolithic. But that itself was nothing new; many of the changes that we trace were the result of established communities picking up on new ideas and new resources.

Given the short chronologies and political sensibilities of his time, it is not surprising that Collingwood saw change arising from distinctive folk movements and usually from without. There wasn't really room for things to be more fluid. For us, the picture is more confusing. The evidence is patchy, often no more than scatters of worked stone in ploughed fields and beach deposits. What there is, however, indicates that a pattern of small and scattered communities already established in the Mesolithic continued into the following period, the signature strongest along the coast where wind and water bring worked stone to the surface. As Collingwood himself suggested, woodlands were a common context for many aspects of life. The Mesolithic had seen people actively manipulate and manage woodlands and this seems to have continued into the Neolithic. There were continuities in more specific patterns of settlement too, around places like Williamson's Moss, St Bees or Ravenglass to name but a few. Scatters containing stone tools and waste from both periods suggest that some areas were used over long sequences, probably in episodes. It was also small scale, certainly not what we now mean when we say 'village', comprising no more than an extended family or two. There were times and places where people came together in greater numbers and others where company was yet more tightly drawn; life was varied and the seasons made different demands. But for much of the time, the company people kept was close, defined by blood ties, by shared tasks and other forms of kinship.[15] Those who kept the same clearings or followed the same paths along the valley sides of the Duddon, the Waver or the Ellen, the Irt or the Esk.

Some of this sounds familiar, not a million miles from the caricature of small pastoral families that fed the Romantic vision in the early nineteenth century. But like that vision, it is largely a product of the focus we adopt; the boundaries we put up. In Cumbria in the fifth and fourth millennia BC, scattered communities also recognised themselves as part of extensive webs of kinship and affiliation. These networks found expression when paths overlapped, in the names given to prominent features, in stories of distant places and in the origin myths that were traced in the land.[16] This was a time when the cycles of the wild, the needs of stock and other matters often encouraged periodic movement – along a varied and changing coast or up the valley; even onto higher ground. Contact with others was an expectation or a requirement of certain tasks. Tenure went in step with this, rather more blurred than the exclusive sense of property we recognise today.[17] Communities of the time had strong attachments to the land and to particular places, ties understood in historic, practical and even spiritual terms. But connections were not always based upon their continuous presence, nor on the absence of others. Ranges overlapped, a crossing of paths encouraged by the physical variety of the land itself.

This larger web was also realised through trade and exchange; the keeping of trading partners and the giving of gifts – rooted in an ethos of sharing that had long been common on the trail, the circulation of goods bound people together. It was also a form of politics, a medium through which new relations could be forged and old ties reworked as one year or one generation gave way to another. It was through these shifting networks that people, materials and ideas circulated beyond the watersheds and ranges of particular communities. And it was most likely through them that some of the materials and ideas that we call Neolithic were encountered. Not a wave of advance, but minor currents which took different paths in and out of the area.[18]

Perspective was different. People did not share the bird's-eye view that we take for granted today.[19] They did not see Cumbria, England or Britain, neither the geography nor the politics that lies behind those names. Their ways of seeing were situated, from certain points of view. Scales changed as they moved and met with others; a shifting in and out of focus between local and more distant concerns. And though the physical geography of the area lent itself to particular ways of dwelling, it was not entirely bounded. The web extended beyond more recent county lines and even across the water.

Far from being the boundary that we have recognised for the last few centuries, the Irish Sea lay at the heart of life. It was an excellent medium for movement and communication, up and down the coast, and across to the Isle of Man and Ireland. A routine ebb and flow of people was a basic fact of life, communication traceable today in shared architectural traits and in the character of artefacts across a broad area. This included stone axes, which were carried in both directions across the water. Names, relations and other concerns no doubt changed from one valley system and from one part of the region to another. You could probably catch it in the sound of a voice as much as in what was being said. But always there were currents that carried you beyond those day-to-day horizons, talk that turned on stories of the distant, of origins and connections.[20]

The sea also had its seasons. Not far on the map, it is rather different from the shore or from a dugout. It is also changeable; winter brought horizons down on water just as it did on land. Fog could claim the coast, just as clouds took the higher peaks. There were times when communication was difficult and dangerous and even when conditions were right, a journey along the coast or further out required knowledge of tides, currents and landmarks. And the water could still turn against you. It is not hard to imagine that beyond what people said of those on the other side, the journey itself was a potent act, featuring in stories of origin and of long dead kin. It required skill and it required fortune; one taken on board as one moved through life, the other perhaps encouraged by rituals of departure and return. Perhaps it was even important that the journey back and forth to what we call Ireland followed the rise, arc and fall of the sun.

The sea brings things to shore by accident as well as by design. To talk of the beginnings of the Neolithic as a colonial wave of advance would be to miss the currents that pulled things in different directions. It was in these more fluid conditions that communities began to experiment with stock and crops, some

indigenous, others brought in with the ebb and flow of people. Older relationships with the wild did not vanish with the arrival of the first domesticates. Hunting still mattered, as did the learning of the skills that this involved – the making and using of certain tools, tracking and understanding your relation to game. Gathering continued too, in woodlands and in the marshes of broad estuaries, customary stands visited from one year to the next. There was still a rich and varied crop to be had. Yet in taking stock and other things besides, communities came to rework old values, a process which would eventually change the character and perception of the land. Stone axes were an intimate part of that process:

> Less than a year ago Mr John Quayle, the tenant of Ehenside, proposed to drain a sheet of water extending over about four or five acres and to add the land thus reclaimed to his farm. He dug a sluice fifteen feet deep and drew the water off to the river; and thus the basin, if not quite dry, was at any rate, fully exposed to observation. . . Along the shore and continued round within a few yards of the water mark, was a line of white stones, burned white by the action of fire. Along with these, there was a very large quantity of charcoal, burnt wood, broken twigs, nuts and leaves, and some few, but not many, broken and charred bones of wild cattle and perhaps deer. Stone and flint implements, such as axes, knives and chisels, were plentiful, still not one trace of iron, bronze or metal of any kind has come to light. The rude and primeval people whose existence these relics indicate were only in possession of implements of flint and stone . . .

So wrote the Revd J.W. Kenworthy in the *Whitehaven Herald* in 1870, the first account of discoveries made at Ehenside Tarn near Sellafield. In the following year, R.D. Darbishire (Esq. B.A.; F.G.S) returned to the Tarn to undertake more controlled excavations.[21] He recovered more Neolithic implements, including several 'felstone' axes, some unfinished, together with grinding stones, pottery, querns and other artefacts. These were accompanied by an organic assemblage that had only survived because of the wet conditions.[22] A tangle of brush and trees were identified, among them oak, birch, hazel and beech, which had fallen into the tarn, reflecting something of the setting, which Darbishire calls 'forest bog'. Remarkably, the preserved wood included a haft in which a stone blade was still in place, together with another in poorer condition. There were also what he describes as wooden paddles and clubs, which now survive as engravings.

Despite well over a century of work since then and many questions left hanging, the Tarn remains one of the better known Neolithic sites in the region. It also draws together the threads that make up this book. The place is a reminder that more recent drainage and deep ploughing have bitten

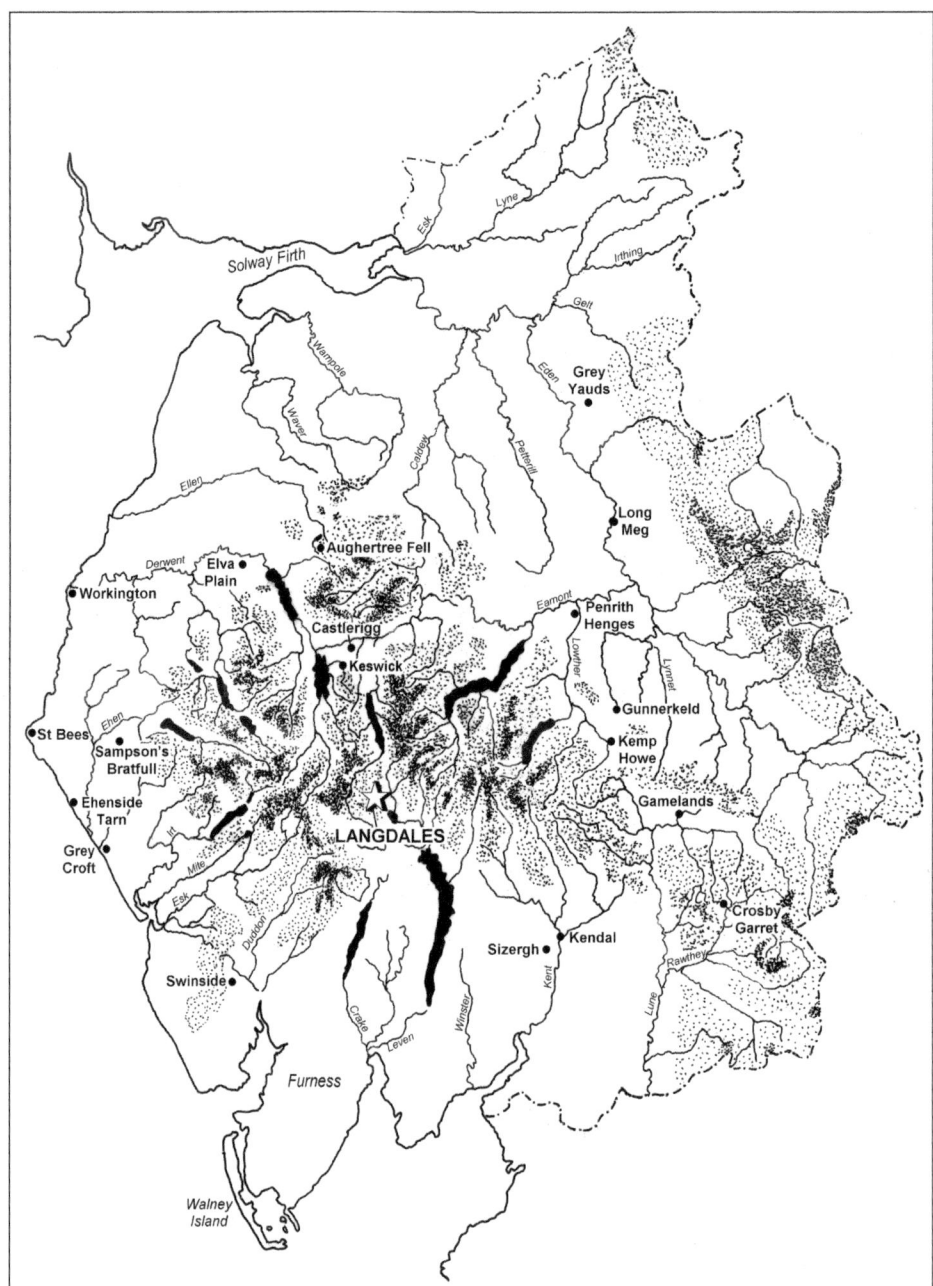

deeply, that the land has changed; improvement just one step in a longer process. Just how that process has unfolded around the Langdales is something we will try to follow. The names and titles of the authors also give a flavour of a social context of enquiry, of interests that were particular to a certain time and to a certain class. The way of seeing we associate with the Picturesque and with the Romantic cult of the mountains is no different. The projection

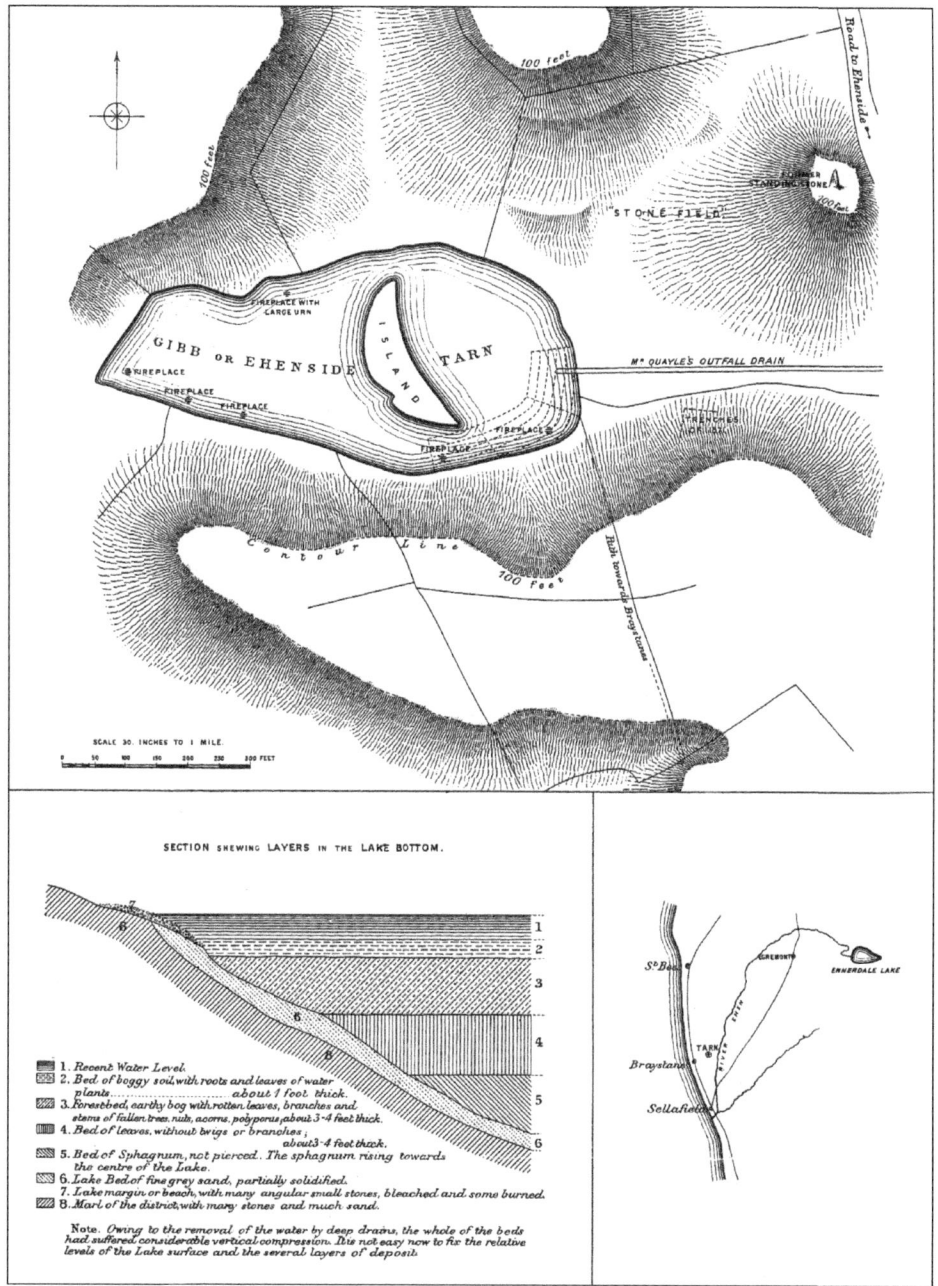

Excavations at Ehenside Tarn. Darbishire 1873. Society of Antiquaries of London

still has a powerful influence, but it has only ever been one point of view amongst many. The poet never trod entirely 'where the sower dwelt', their paths just crossed. If there is a general point to be drawn, it is that there have always been many ways of engaging with and understanding the area. Different ways of seeing that have overlapped with class and gender, with

A way in. Above the track from Blea Tarn. Photo: Geoffrey Berry

ethnicity and more besides, perspectives shaped by biography and by experience. Tracking some of that variety – in the present and the past – is a necessary part of the task.

That is what makes places like Ehenside Tarn or the crags of the Langdales so fascinating and so difficult to understand. At Ehenside, the sodden trunks and timbers give a glimpse of very different conditions to those we take for granted today. Hearths strung out near the edge of the water, a tangle of understorey and trees. Down the trail there are other clearings where crops are being grown, and beyond them, other trails to the high ground and to the sea. People are sat around their fires or bent over stones, a small company engaged in talk and in grinding, finishing and hafting blades. In their hands are axes made of a rock won from the Langdales, a journey of several days to the east. What follows is an attempt to explore what it meant to be a part of those conditions; how the knot of people at the water's edge understood themselves and the land around them. Most of all, it is an attempt to understand just how and why they made that journey; to catch, if that is possible, what the crags meant to people long before the invention of the Sublime.

CHAPTER 2

AN EXTENSION OF THE HAND

Stone celts are held to preserve from lightning the house in which they are kept. They perspire when a storm is approaching; they are good for diseases of man and beast; they increase the milk of cows; they assist the birth of children; and powder scraped from them may be taken with some advantage for various childish disorders. It is usually nine days after their fall before they are found on the surface. . . [1]

Axe: a noun and a verb. Something to work with, something to grind, an action, a transformation. A simple word with more than one meaning. Stone axes turn up everywhere. Some come to light in excavations, but most are found as stray finds; brought to the surface by the plough, on pipelines or in the foundations of new buildings. Others turn up on beck sides or footpaths, where water or walking boots have cut into fresh earth. Axes were not unique to the Neolithic. People had been making and using them across the Mesolithic, certainly for thousands of years. There is also evidence that some were probably circulated between people.[2] Most of these were made of flint or similar materials, and were flaked into shape with a hammer of stone or antler. A few, made on mudstones, schists and other river cobbles were also ground to a finer form, their cutting edges smoothed by hours of patient working. It was not, however, until the Neolithic that the use of distinct sources and the grinding of axes became a persistent, widespread and important concern. In Cumbria, this began in the decades around 4000 BC and left its clearest mark on crags around the Langdales.

The Langdales

THUNDERBOLTS AND WONDERS

The recent history of stone axes is a chequered one. Just over a hundred years ago, people were routinely placing them in water troughs to guarantee the health of their stock, or using them as talismans of protection against the elements. Once recognised as elf-shot or as the shards of spent thunderbolts, their presence in the rafters was thought to ward off lightning on the grounds that it never struck the same place twice. They still grace many mantelpieces and for as many different reasons. Axes have also been prominent in accounts of prehistory, where they have gone by many names. Referred to as 'celts', the term a derivation of the Latin for chisel, and as 'shoe last' adzes or axes because of their resemblance to a cobbler's pattern. A keystone in the foundation of archaeology, they have loomed large in the disciplinary imagination ever since, a fossil of particular periods and a touchstone for arguments about the character of society over time.

Just when axes started to be collected is impossible to say. Even in prehistory, old blades were sometimes relics worthy of curation. They certainly caught the eye of classical scholars, who speculated at length about their

Axes of flint and stone. Museum of Archaeology and Anthropology, University of Cambridge

meteoric or celestial origins, sometimes finding omens in their discovery. Axes were no less important in the medieval imagination, gracing collections of marvels in the hands of wealthy merchants. From the eighteenth century onwards, they were prized by collectors; aristocrats and gentlemen of taste and learning, who set them in cabinets of curiosities alongside fossils and other wonders. The ordering of things was different then, our disciplinary divisions not yet formed. An axe might be found next to a Narwhal tusk, or an ammonite, a nautilus shell or a mummified hand. Sir Walter Scott had a battered 'stone celt' in a cabinet at his home, where it lay, amongst other things, cheek by jowl with a lock of Nelson's hair and a piece of bread from the sporran of a clansman fallen on the field at Bannockburn.

These cabinets were neither random nor meaningless. They were of their time and often personal. Acquisition and ownership was a mark of learned interest, as much a mark of standing amongst the polite as a grasp of the Sublime. A good cabinet and collection reflected well upon its owner. And chaotic though it may seem to us, there was an order to things. Sometimes personal and fetishistic, sometimes tied to broader attitudes, early collections were tentative journeys into a changing world; attempts to make sense of nature and the diversity of humanity appropriated by expanding empires. An axe could take many paths to the cabinet: recovered from newly improved land nearby; a gift from a grateful cleric who had excavated an old barrow on the estate; an object that invited comparisons with tools returned from the colonies. Sometimes it was no more than the distinctive colour or the fossil that could be traced within a form.[3]

As the nineteenth century unfolded, these strange assemblages gave way to more familiar orders. Polite fashions moved on and disciplines coalesced around agreed objects of study. Lines were drawn between different fields – botany, geology, archaeology; nature on the one hand and culture on the other. Like a child who discards a private hoard once they are schooled, many cabinets were reorganised or donated to become the foundations of the museum collections of today. Scholars of the time asked new questions of the objects before them. As interest in evolutionary processes grew; artefacts such as axes took on a new importance for what they could be made to say about the character of human societies at particular stages of development. Description became more formal and conventional, establishing categories that are still recognised today. Using principles of stratigraphy and the evidence from a burgeoning excavation record, particular types of axe were identified and assigned a place in chronological sequences. Distinctions were drawn between those made of flint, much of it from the chalklands of the south and east, and those made of stone from glacial erratics and the varied geologies of northern and western Britain. Along with other tools, ground and polished axes became *fossiles directeurs*, associated first with the Stone Age and then exclusively with the more recent Neolithic phase.

The intention, outcome and milieu of this work is captured in the introduction to Sir John Evans' *The Ancient Stone Implements of Great Britain*. Published in 1872, it was the culmination of what Evans describes as 'the occupation of what leisure hours I could spare'. The second edition, published in 1897, runs to a leisurely 747 pages:

> In the following pages I purpose to give an account of the various forms of stone implements, weapons and ornaments of remote antiquity discovered in Great Britain, and their probable uses and method of manufacture, and also, in some instances, the circumstances of their discovery. While reducing the whole series into some form of classification, as has been done for the stone antiquities of Scandinavia by Worsaae, Montelius and Sophus Müller, for those of France by Messrs Gabriel and Adrien de Mortillet, and for those of Ireland by Sir William Wilde, I hope to add something to our knowledge of this branch of Archaeology by instituting comparisons, where possible, between the antiquities of England and Scotland and those other parts of the world. Nor in considering the purposes to which the various forms were applied, and the method of their manufacture, must I neglect to avail myself of the illustrations afforded by the practice of modern savages, of which Sir John Lubbock and others have already made such profitable use. . . [4]

The language of this statement says a good deal about the intellectual climate of the time. Evans moved in circles where technological innovation was seen as progressive, as the driving force of social change. From that perspective, axes were important symbols. Regarded as an advance on the flaked tools of earlier times, ground stone axes were arranged in serried ranks on the shelves of museums. There they stood, on parade, testaments to the level of technical accomplishment achieved by Neolithic farmers on their march towards civilisation and the (western) present. They became icons of improvement, tools developed to clear the wilderness and establish an order to land that scholars of the time could recognise and call familiar. Much of the language used between the late nineteenth century and the 1920s bore more than a passing resemblance to the ways that early colonists had talked about their 'taming' of the New World.

An important current in these arguments was the encounter with cultural traditions outside of the West. As European empires consolidated their hold on many parts of the world, ethnography and the growing appetite for collection brought scholars of the past into contact with the material conditions of other people's lives. In the crude evolutionary schemes of the time, these encounters were powerful. Here were people making and using similar tools to those found on archaeological sites in Europe. It was as if time rolled back the further one travelled from the museums and salons of Copenhagen, London or Paris.

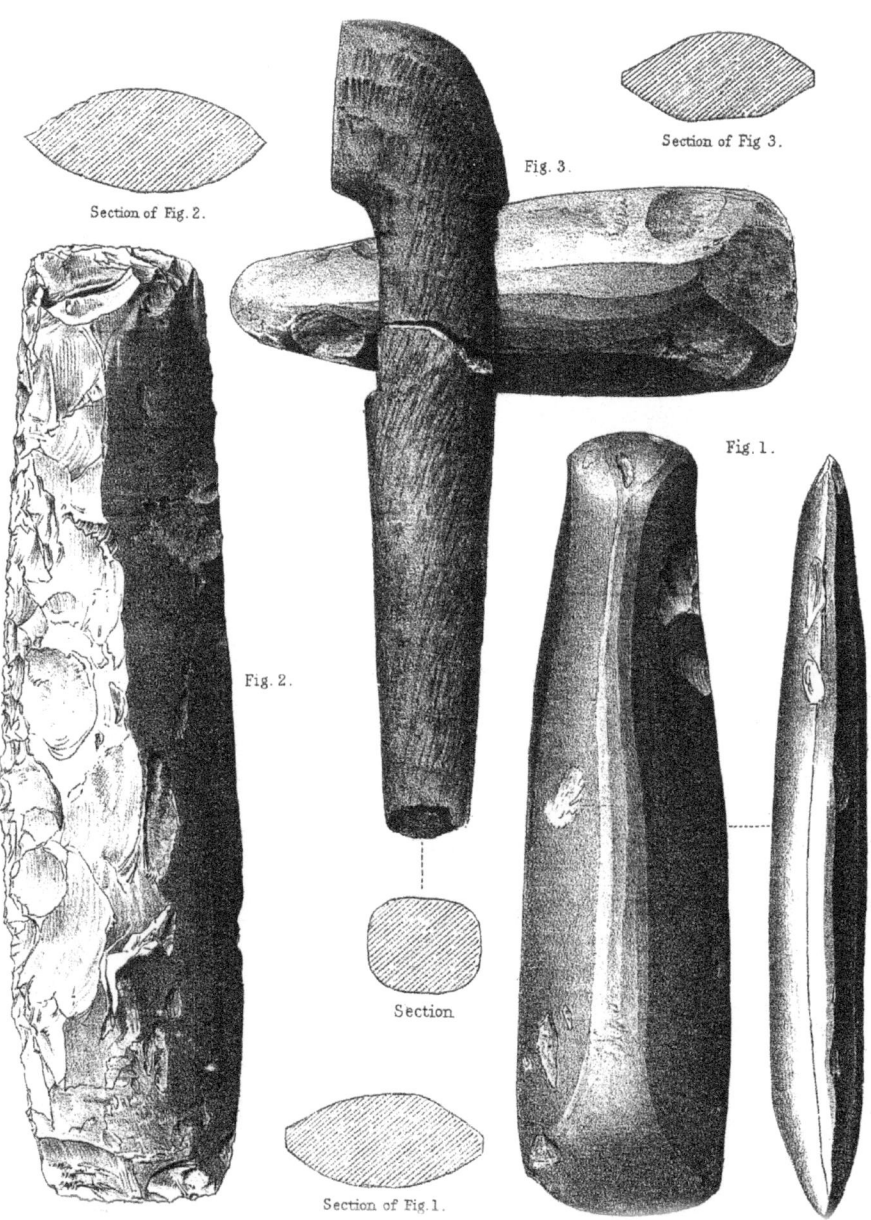

Implements recovered from Ehenside Tarn. Darbishire 1873. Society of Antiquaries of London

Collections were swelled by artefacts from distant lands, curated and placed alongside those recovered closer to home – axes from Australia, Pitcairn Island or Papua New Guinea side by side with those from Cumbria or North Wales. Many remain in collections today, washed up against the shores of early museums and given new meanings. In this intellectual climate, parallels were commonly drawn to infer the function of prehistoric axes and other tools. But people often went further than that. Artefacts became indices against which to measure the complexity of particular societies, past and present. Nowhere was this clearer than in the museum established at Oxford by Augustus Pitt Rivers. Mapping the contemporary mindset on the walls, he arranged artefacts according to their perceived sophistication, the resulting tableaux taken as a reflection of socio-evolutionary processes at work. Simple to Complex: Savage to Modern.

Much of this way of thinking is now rejected, not least because it doesn't work, but also because it has often served, some might say continues to serve, a more sinister purpose. The idea that distance in space and succession in time were somehow equivalent was easily recruited to sustain a pernicious 'myth of primitivism'; that societies outside of the west were somehow further back down a ladder of social evolution. On the back of disease and military force, such arguments were used to justify the exploitation of people who, denied their own identity, were classified as simple equivalents for the denizens of European prehistory.[5]

> Quite obviously these axes are implements requiring great pains to perfect and on which an enormous amount of labour was often expended not merely for utilitarian purposes but also to satisfy aesthetic feeling, the product, in a word, of a progressive and capable folk. . .[6]

As the century progressed, the appetite for axes was considerable, even voracious. Curators and collectors across the country would pay good money for complete and aesthetically pleasing examples. Individuals and institutions sometimes competed for the archives of particularly important sites, and assemblages were occasionally divided to satisfy obligations or establish academic bonds. Whatever they meant when first made and used, axes were given new values, even serving as gifts. Many of the blades found in Cumbria and elsewhere were picked up in the wake of the plough and of development; early accounts talk of discoveries while trenching or cutting through peat. Most are recorded as isolated finds, though some were found in association with others. In the 1860s, a group of three 'celts of dark green felsite', were recovered during drainage works at Belmont near Penrith, another cluster found in Wigton in much the same way.[7] At Portinscale, the cutting of fishponds brought as many as seven blades to light, several 'laid along by the side of the trunk of a small oak tree' preserved beneath the peat. Just how and why these groups came to be deposited is difficult to say. Some may have been cached for later recovery, or were left on working floors. Others may have been more deliberate hoards, deposits a result of more considered acts of interrment. This may have been the case at Skelmore Heads, near Ulverston, where four flaked stone blades were found in 1959 in a gryke or fissure in the limestone, 'thrust into the crevice as a compact bundle'.

Recovery was also encouraged by the final stages of enclosure, a fresh crop of artefacts brought to the surface as land was cleared, drained and put to the plough for the first time. Labourers on many farms added to their meagre incomes by selling these pieces and were sometimes even given training. At Fimber in East Yorkshire, John and Robert Mortimer gave instructions on identification and even issued handbills which offered financial and other rewards. Many others did the same, travelling from farm to farm offering payment in coin or kind.[8] On a scale not seen since the Neolithic, axes flowed from rediscovered 'manufactories' and from other settings, swelling the inventories of collections across the country. Reporting to the Royal Society of Antiquaries of Ireland in 1906, William Knowles noted meeting local antiquarians whilst removing one of several cartloads of axes from the source at Tievebulliagh, County Antrim.[9]

Not all blades were as old as they appeared. The archives of many museums contain references to fakes, and in several areas, demand was met by local farmers, who became adept at turning out copies, some with stone handles, to sell to visitors. On occasion, this was actively encouraged. In the later nineteenth century, Edward Simpson – 'Flint Jack' – was popular at society lectures, where he would be called upon to demonstrate the skills of ancient stoneworking. He could also make a sort of living producing artefacts that would sometimes pass as originals. He was not the only one. Working for profit and sometimes at the instigation of archaeologists, people like William Smith – 'Skin and Grief' – in East Yorkshire or 'Billy Nummer' in Suffolk turned out many artefacts that went on to grace the pages of learned journals and the display cases of museums. Not all of their handiwork can be traced:

> . . . they have . . . long, narrow proportions, lateral facets, the maximum width usually being about the middle of the implement and not at the cutting edge and a distinct 'waisting', or constriction, towards the butt end which is sometimes squared and often ground to an edge. . .[10]

The legacy of these older traditions of fascination and enquiry remains with us today. We still draw the same basic lines; between flaked and ground axes, and between flint and other raw materials. Interest in form has also continued, with Clare Fell probably the most important contributor to the study of axe

The Langdales

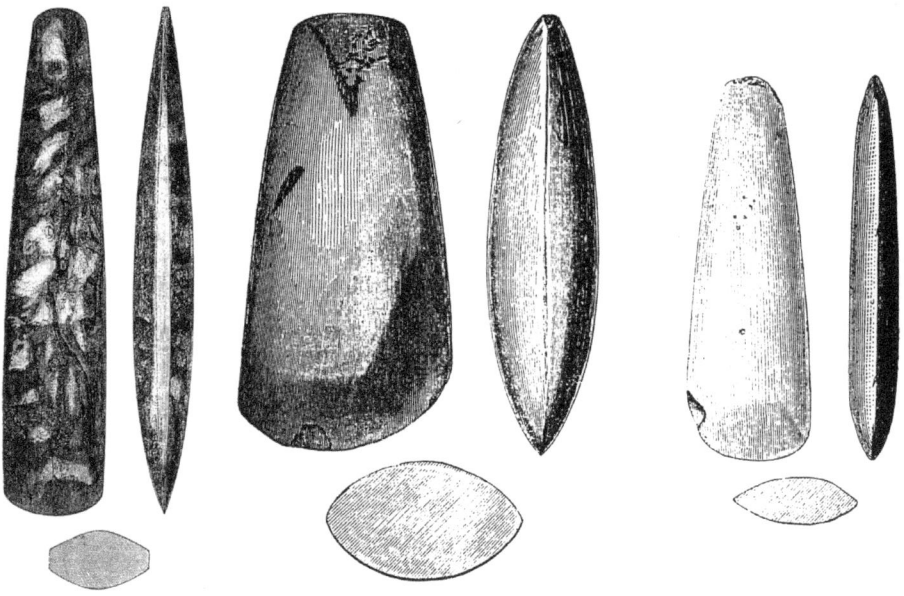

morphology in Cumbria. One of the more significant developments has been the fingerprinting of different groups of stone artefacts and the tracing of these back to their points of geological origin.[11] One of the early successes in this work was the linking of a specific petrological group of axes (known in the literature as Group VI) with outcropping volcanic sources in the central Cumbrian Fells. Identified closely though not exclusively with the Langdales, work on implements made from this distinctive volcanic tuff produced startling results. Many were found within the region; from small, heavily worn and reworked axes to larger and more elaborate forms – so called 'Cumbrian Clubs'. But many more were found at greater distances; in Lancashire, over the Pennines, in Scotland, Ireland and across much of central and southern Britain.[12] Similar spreads were seen from other sources; from Tievebulliagh in Ireland, Mounts Bay in Cornwall and Graig Lwyd in North Wales. There were even axes which originated on the continent; mottled flint from Scandinavia and jadeite from alpine sources.[13]

The extraordinary scale of these distributions prompted many responses. From the middle of the twentieth century, people began to talk of an 'axe trade', and of the development of industries centred on 'factories', where Neolithic quarrymen laboured full time to satisfy the demands of a national market. Parallels were drawn with the early flint mines of the south, and it was assumed that these places operated in a similar manner. If there had been a 'Queen's Award for Industry' back then, no doubt the crest would have been mounted near the top of the Pikes.[14]

Nowadays, we are not so sure. Radiocarbon dating suggests that axes were made, used and circulated for much of the Neolithic, a span of up to two

An Extension of the Hand

thousand years. Our distributions could easily reflect a more gradual and piecemeal pattern of dispersal than was once envisaged. We also know that across Britain as a whole, people made axes from locally available material; from outcrops of flint where they occurred, and from glacial erratics, stones carried from their geological points of origin by successive waves of ice.[15] The picture is certainly more blurred than was once supposed. More basic still, we now question whether an image of labour derived from modern industrial experience really does justice to how axes were perceived or how working was organised at the time. Things may have been quite different.

> *How old did you say; five thousand? I can't believe it. . . It was just there sticking out of the stream bank, that's it. . . It feels good just turning it over in my hand. . . is it worth anything?*

TOKENS OF IDENTITY

So what were axes for? How were they used and what did they mean to communities of the time? As used by archaeologists, the term itself is a shorthand and can be misleading. We seldom recover axes, just the durable

Gavrinis, Brittany. After Shee Twohig 1981

stone blades. Wooden hafts are rare and survive only in exceptional conditions such as those encountered at Ehenside Tarn or Solway Moss.[16] The term is also a shorthand in another way. We often talk of axes when it would be more accurate to say adze, chisel, wedge or hoe. Sometimes the shape of individual examples, the scars that they bear, or the manner of their hafting suggest a wider variety of uses than the name normally allows.

Axes were ubiquitous. They could be used in many tasks and where necessary, could be hafted and rehafted to serve different purposes. When edges broke or became dull through use, they could be resharpened or refashioned, blades reducing in size and changing in shape, just as people's bodies changed over the course of their lives. Slung over the shoulder they may have gone almost unnoticed as people moved, as they worked or talked with one another. A hafted axe could even be something to sit on while pausing on the trail. Some also saw use or potential as weapons, turned against others in the face of tensions between communities – arguments over access to pasture or to sacred sites, rustling or bad blood that had simmered for years.

It was this remarkable potential that led many to talk of axes as an 'extension of the hand', but the connection was never just mechanical. Working involved a relationship with tools just as it involved a relationship with other people. Things became recognised and familiar. They fitted into particular hands more closely than others, and over time, connections were made which were as much biography as they were utility. And those relationships grew as people worked with particular tools, refashioning, sharpening and attending to them as they went on. Tools might even outlive their owners, handed down between generations.[17] Where this happened they carried not just a potential for use, but connections with others and with the past; a patina of personal history. In the oral cultures of the time, axes were not just extensions of the hand, they were extensions of identity.

> *. . . the walking stick? . . . It was my mother's before I picked it up at the back door . . . I'm the same height . The badges are from trips she took with dad before I was born . . . the Cairngorms, the Lakes, the Alps, all over the place . . . My boys don't believe it, even when I show them the photos . . .*

There are several lines of evidence that axes were more than hardware. Blades from regions like Cumbria have been found in other parts of Britain which were rich in raw materials. If stone and skill were readily available, why did some move over such great distances? There are also the blades themselves. Many show signs of extensive and protracted use. Battered and irregular cutting edges, flake scars that slice through a ground surface, snapped blades and so on. But there are blades in many regions that would have been useless. Some are either too small or too large to have been wielded effectively. A few have been perforated and may have been suspended as pendants. And there are some

An Extension of the Hand

which are so thin, highly polished and delicate that use on anything harder than soft cheese would have caused them to shatter immediately. Even where blades could be used, the extent to which people spent time shaping, grinding and polishing went far beyond necessity. Often, the level of finish was more concerned with bringing out the colour of particular stones, or with the definition of distinctive and recognisable forms. Function was not the only issue.

Other clues can be added to this list. Representations of axes are one of the most common motifs to be found in the carvings found on Neolithic monuments in several parts of western Europe.[18] The axe was sufficiently important as a symbol that its image was carved again and again. Some standing stones with pecked surfaces were themselves representations of monumental axes, their cutting edges biting deep into the earth. The resemblance went beyond appearance. Collective acts of stone dressing involved techniques that mimicked those used to fashion axes from a number of raw materials. Spectacular deposits of elaborate and sometimes exotic axes have also been found in or near to many of these settings, and there are hints of similar concerns in Britain. Axe blades have been found in tombs, in ceremonial enclosures and in pits. In each case, these items were singled out and accorded special treatment, handled and sometimes buried as a feature of important rites. Some were even deliberately broken or smashed as part of this process.[19] Axes have also been recovered from springs and bogs, and in considerable numbers

from rivers trawled by dredgers.[20] Accident and chance loss might account for some of these, but the pattern is a strong one; many were deliberately thrown into the water or placed out of reach.

Axes were not the only objects to be given special treatment. But why were they important? Many tasks and much of life revolved around concerns that had gone unchanged since the Mesolithic. So why should the Neolithic be associated with new sources, new techniques and new forms of attention? There is no simple answer, no single cause to be identified. Farming and practical demand played a part; the role of the axe in acting upon and changing the land contributed to the way it was regarded. But the emergence of new ways of thinking about land and time was just as crucial. What we can say is that the fourth millennium saw a sharpening of focus on the axe as a token of identity. Making and using them spoke in subtle ways about who people were, the places that they occupied in the community and in the broader landscapes of the time – the stone, the source, the skill in making and using; all of these mattered. Many have suggested that axes were associated with concepts of maleness and adulthood, and though they were probably used by a variety of people, it is likely that these links were recognised. These were not new concerns in themselves. Differences of age, gender and of kinship had always mattered as had other senses of affiliation and belonging. What changed in the fourth millennium was the medium through which some of these concerns were addressed.

Axes were statements in stone, acknowledged in passing, on the shoulder, in use and in talk. They built up biographies and associations and some may even have had names. It was this potential that came into focus when they were singled out for special attention: held aloft or handled as cues in the telling of stories or the recitation of names; treated like those they had lived alongside, buried or broken just as bodies were. Deposition could mark a connection with a place, the end of a relationship, the 'burying of the hatchet' or the invocation of spirits who required a gift. That may be why they were thrown into rivers; pathways to other places but also to other worlds. Perhaps the story of Excalibur had very ancient roots indeed.

Something to work with, something to grind, something to speak of at certain times. Because they carried people with them, axe blades were well suited as tokens for exchange, circulated in the playing out of relations between communities. In a world where identity was bound up in the possession and use of things, the circulation of axes was crucial to the renewal of ties between scattered groups. But before that could happen, they had to be made.

CHAPTER 3

WOODWORK

Mostly ash and elm, sometimes willow or oak depending on where you are – you don't always notice them at first. The eye slips easily between bare branches to the fellside beyond, and it is only when the light changes that they come into focus. Pollards are scattered all over the Langdale valley. Solitary sentries near the road, others in line along the becks, a few clinging to the edges of ghylls that boil down the slopes after a storm. Some still thrive, but many are dead or dying; bark gone, trunks polished by the wind. Uncut rods have grown beyond customary sizes, spraying out in all directions, a few branches breathing a last gasp of small green shoots. Crowns that raised a hard fist to the sky are puckered now by the rot of water and mould that collects between the knuckles. In some, the rot has worked its way down, the growth rings of youth eaten away. The outer timber curls around the hollow.

Pollarding was a familiar activity around Langdale. Practiced on oak, ash, elm and willow amongst others, it involved cutting back a tree to foster a crown above head height. New growth was encouraged from the crown, where it flourished until needed, out of the reach of stock. This provided leafy fodder and thin bark; rods, withies and larger poles for use around the farm. Cropped or topped by 'back bills' or billhooks, pollards were maintained across generations. Crowns swelled above stubby trunks, creating the distinctive shapes that would not look out of place in a painting by Bruegel. Run along a beck, they gave a rich crop, and their vigorous roots helped hold the banks together. In some places, they still do. Cultivated in hedge lines or on wall tops

The Langdales

near a farm, they were ready to hand when heavy snows buried the grazing on which animals relied. Set higher up, beyond the ring garths of isolated farms, they often stood in company as wood pasture, land that could be grazed while new growth flourished overhead. Pollards were important enough that they were sometimes named in inventories, or served as reference points when journeys were described.

Pollarding is not the task it once was. Many of the trees that cling to open fellsides or hide under the cover of birches have not been cut for years. Others now stand isolated in fields, long removed boundaries remembered by the line of major boughs. Where cutting does happen, usually close to home or near the road, it is often at the behest of the National Trust, who see pollards and the act, as important to 'landscape value', to the conservation of appearances that can be traced in old engravings. Guidelines have been written, and there are stories, probably apocryphal, of people brought in to teach skills that have not yet been forgotten. In most places, there simply isn't the need for the harvest.

In the past we would cut branches for them. We would leave the gate open so that they could drop in and as soon as they heard the axe they would come running down the hill . . .

Trees around Tarn Hows, the Langdales in the background

From the time of Thomas West's guide onwards, woodlands were essential to the Lakeland scene.¹ A focus for poets, painters and those who came simply to enjoy the view, they were a required element on the beautiful lower ground, reflected in the lakes or casting their shadows over antiquated hedgerows. They were also a necessary border to the sublime fells above; isolated trees clinging to rocks a favoured subject for a sketch.² Conservation laws now protect many of the deciduous woodlands that give particular dales their character and these are maintained by selective fencing and felling. Many visitors tend to miss the management. They see instead an untouched fellside and draw sharp lines between these stands and the plantations that generate income and controversy in equal measure. Nothing gets collars hotter than dark and serried ranks of larch or spruce.

It has been that way for some time. Since the eighteenth century, when the 'proper' appearance of nature became a sharp concern, debate has focused on the look of the land, tensions rising between economic and aesthetic interests. Even then, distaste was expressed for the cash crops that '. . . grow up into nothing but deformity . . .', an opinion echoed down the years as the scale of planting increased. But many of the landowners building villas at the lakeside were also improvers, people like the Curwens around Windermere, who were cash cropping trees from plantations on their estate from an early stage. These

The Langdales

commercial concerns developed alongside other views. Interest in woodlands tapped into the idea of a 'Greenwood England' which had been a source of national symbolism from at least the sixteenth century.[3] By the eighteenth, the need for wood and timber was so great that driftwood was being brought back from the east coast of America and planting on many estates increased to service the demand. Outside the private parks, where trees were valued for their antiquity, appearance and framing effects, the planting of more regimented woodlands was not just a source of income; it was a patriotic act.[4]

Argument is no less sharp today than it was in the early twentieth century, when the Forestry Commission planted several million trees in central Cumbria in little more than a decade. Planners negotiate their way around exclusion zones from Eskdale to Esthwaite. Others argue for employment, and there is a powerful and justified lobby against monocultures on vast and regimented scales. Positions are easily polarised, and it is common to hear the same line drawn again and again, between nature on the one hand and industry on the other. That line is rather more blurred than we often allow. The working of woodlands has always been important in Cumbria. Employment and subsistence, the basis

Charcoal burning. Photo: Kendal Library

for crafts and for particular ways of living; people's relationships with trees have set much of the pattern that many now value as timeless.

> *This primitive little valley looking like a stretch of Switzerland or one of the German Alp dales, has some importance though in the history of its time, and an economic value to the country at large. For here, buried among trees and in a place of beauty fitter for temple or palace, for parsonage or love cottage, than its present uses – are the Government powder works: the most unlikely of all things to be found in an Alpine valley, where apparently nothing more practical than waterfalls and crags are to be met with. All this side of the country is famous for its charcoal. Richly wooded and for the most part with quick growing timber, rather a large business is kept up in bobbins, cask hoops and staves, bark for tanning, fence wood, charcoal and more rarely, flooring planks and mast wood . . .*[5]

There were many ways of engaging with woodlands, some with ancient roots. The taking of oak bark for tanning, alder burning for potash, the harvesting of building timbers. Alongside more day-to-day uses as fodder and fuel, these and other demands on woodlands required complex rights of access and often led to conflicts of interest. One of the most widespread practices was coppicing. Unlike pollards, coppiced trees were cut close to the ground, stools or boles cultivated for the harvesting of rods and poles. This meant that they often needed protection from animals and walls or banks which served this purpose appear on many early estate maps. Coppice offered fodder from time to time, but its primary purpose was to provide the raw materials for fencing and hurdles, and above all else, for charcoal. For centuries, charcoal was valued as a smelting agent in the working of iron, copper, silver and lead. Before the dissolution, the powerful monastic houses who owned large tracts of the region gave a good deal of land to coppice. Administrative documents from places like Furness Abbey reflect a thriving industry and complex leasing arrangements, metal smelting often set close by. Demand for charcoal expanded again in the post-medieval era. It was an essential element in the working of blast furnaces at places like Duddon and in the powder that was increasingly used for blasting in stone quarries, certain species like juniper being highly prized for their use in fuses.[6] Established in the early nineteenth century, the powder works at Elterwater was one local outcome of this process. Occupying land that is now a timeshare complex and taking water from Stickle Tarn to drive its wheels, the works supplied a local and international market for 'loose' blasting powder.

Coaling was a patient process. Stools were usually harvested for shanklings and coalwood every fifteen years or so; straight poles cut and stacked before being covered by sifted earth and turf. Embers were introduced through a central funnel and the stack would then be tended day and night until the burn was complete. This could take several days and burners usually camped in makeshift dwellings next to the pitstead, judging the state of the process by the smell and the colour of the smoke. Once the stack had been reduced to a half or even a third of its original size, the turf was removed to reveal the 'satin black' of the fuel which was shipped out to hungry furnaces. Many had a hand in coaling. Farmers supplementing incomes with a few pitsteads and nurtured stands, estates reaping rich rewards from leases and from a burgeoning market. And then there were the communities who gave themselves over more completely to the task, set apart during the burning season, cutting and maintaining stools at other times. Families who held leases on particular stretches of coppice and worked these in rotation over many years, handing rights and skills down their line. Though many trees have long since gone, the circular platforms of old pitsteads can still be seen in many dales, blackened soil beneath the turf. There are still a few in Langdale, on the intake land between Harry Place and Millbeck, set close to the water that helped control the burn.

The bleached skeletons and overgrown rods that we see today are the result of ways of working with trees that were as social as they were practical. For the coalers, work set a pattern to life. It coloured their relationships with others, just as it etched their skin. And where rods had to grow for half a generation or more, it encouraged a way of thinking about time that went beyond the here and now. Their perceptions were very different from those of visitors who saw unchanging forest, or those who suspended leases on their land to keep

Elterwater Common. Photo: Geoffrey Berry

the sniff of industry at arms length. We also know from medieval sources that the perception of pollards sometimes broke along the lines that divided people. Wood pastures beyond intakes were generally held in common. Customary rights and sometimes the payment of 'forest silver' or 'dale male', allowed grazing beneath the crowns and the taking of firewood, bracken and fodder.[7] But the common or waste was also the Lord's demesne, land for hunting and an area often rich in minerals and valuable building timber to which they laid claim. To cut regularly or to set new pollards meant stunting the overall growth of trees and this, like bites of enclosure into the common, led sometimes to disputes. In the court rolls and agreements that document these concerns, there is a sense of ways of working and of seeing, tied closely to identity.

Perceptions also broke along other lines. For as far back as we have records, people often saw more than just a collection of resources. Woods and forests were frequently regarded as places of danger and uncertainty. Sagas and other medieval sources often depicted them as animate and powerful forces, and these views had a profound influence on the imaginations of later Romantics and Pre-Raphaelites.[8] There were mischievous and more malevolent spirits, trees and groves held as sacred, dark snares to snag the traveller. Even time could work differently amongst the watchful trees. A place to be feared and respected, a place of transformation. It was wilderness too, an image of retreat cultivated and manipulated by religious orders such as the Cistercians. It was not for nothing that Shakespeare often cast the forest as a place of misrule. It was liminal ground, a place between, to enter at one's peril, where the order of things might be inverted. The threat of wild animals and of people who lived outside convention. All these things and more, before it was recast as Arcadia.

It is difficult today to picture just how extensive woodlands once were, or how often they expanded and contracted. It is even harder to explore how they were worked and perceived. Though the filter of our times encourages us to see things as stable and unchanging, the land was far from static. Things shifted; within specific dales and across more extensive areas, the scale and pace of change a product of ownership, industry and ideology. Many see the fells and assume that they have always been clear, missing the fact that they are artefacts of grazing. Take the sheep away and there would soon be scrub on the slopes; birches taking hold amongst rowan and oak. Around the Langdales this has happened several times; the cover advancing and retreating according to the intensity of grazing between the tenth and eighteenth centuries. In the wake of foot-and-mouth and a shift of markets, this is once again a pressing concern. Things have become so difficult in places that some flocks are grazed as much to maintain appearances as for meat or wool; farming a sort of countryside curatorship.

The same is true of lower dales that now lie green and open, the pasture obscuring centuries of industry and arable. Many were home to dark and tangled woodlands well into the first millennium AD, and even when the cover was opened, clearance was not always permanent. There are references to forests in medieval and later documents, including some, like Grizedale, with royal associations. These suggest extensive tracts, though 'forest' is an ambiguous term, and can refer to open country as well as trees. Many Cumbrian place names also end in '-thwaite', a term traceable to Old Norse and to the centuries around AD 1000.[9] It refers to clearings and sometimes to meadows or paddocks and the fact it is so widespread is a hint that woodlands were common in many areas at this time. Clearance, regeneration and working were basic facts of life.

> *. . . what's wrong with this [plantation] then? The ones with just the spruce were ugly I grant you, they went too far . . . too big . . . all them straight lines. But there's a mix of species coming through and it's different now . . . Anyway, it's been going on for hundreds of years, doesn't that count for something . . . We've got charcoal and coppice on the go . . . loads of people coming in . . . Say what you like, there's jobs and money for the area . . .*

The best vantage for the longer view is in the peat that blankets parts of the high country. As in many uplands, the bogs that hang above the Langdale valley have

On the Stickle Ghyll path. Photo: Kendal Library

themselves been worked – a primary source of fuel in the medieval and earlier post-medieval periods and probably before. You can still trace the straight lines and sodden depressions in the peat across areas like Martcrag Moor, even stumble into them when looking elsewhere. The right of turbary was exercised extensively, requiring payment to the landowner and agreement amongst the valley community on where and how often turves could be cut. Individual farms held rights that needed to be maintained and some cuttings served several families; cooperative decisions and working a basis for relations. Fuel also had to be brought downhill and numerous sledways are still traceable; around Troughton Beck and above Raw Head to the east of Scale Gill. Peat also required storage and drying, and there are many peat huts surviving in various stages of dereliction, almost all of them on the northern side of the valley where the sun, when it appears, tends to fall for longer. There are two below Raw Pike, another on Wormal Crag and a cluster near Scale Gill.

We now cut peat for different reasons. Cores through these bogs and through upland and lowland tarns reveal a stratigraphy of peat and sediment containing relict pollen. These provide an index of how much things have changed and are one of the few windows that we have on the pattern of the vegetation in the Neolithic. The evidence is patchy, as was life. But it suggests a rich variety to woodland cover in many areas, a pattern that even then, was far from static. What is clear is that the Neolithic did not witness the wholesale clearance or transformation of the land. The image of a 'wilderness improved' by the sudden, widespread and definitive removal of trees finds little expression in the pollen. In fact, the conditions encountered by small and dispersed kin groups were as varied as they had been during the later Mesolithic. Things changed, they always had. But change was piecemeal and fragmented; it grew out of rather than broke with the past.

Extensive broadleaf tracts were common in many areas; on lower ground and high up the sides of most upland dales. In some areas, the tree line was as high as 750m, a cover of birch, alder and oak, and beyond, a shifting edge of scrub. Hazel, poplar and willow also flourished; conditions very different to the open moorlands of today. A cut through the deeper peats of Langdale Combe reveals the contrast; the stained and softened skeletons of prehistoric brushwood and boughs.[10] There was also open country, just as there had been since the slow retreat of the ice. Coarse grasses whistling beyond the forest margins, the hog-backed spines of open ridges rising up to meet a plateau. Only the hardiest could find a foothold on the steeper crags and trees often skirted mobile screes and wetter or more acid ground. Those on the trail or following game would have looked down onto dales that were mostly thick and dark with cover, eyes following the line of a path or the occasional twisted thread of smoke.[11] Most upland dales were somewhere on the way, not persistently settled at this time. Where the bite of winter could be sharp and snows particularly deep, these higher ranges had a season.

Things were just as varied on the lower slopes and terraces where the high ground met the plains, a presence reflected by a thin spread of monuments and by the chance recovery of artefacts; an axe in a beckside or a flint scatter in a newly ploughed field. Across the forelands and down to the coast, small communities were scattered across the area, moving in and out by land and by sea. Areas thick with understorey gave way to open canopies, varied conditions for animals and people. Around tarns and estuaries there was carr, reed swamp, salt marshes and raised bogs, certain species dominating on heavier and wetter soils behind the sands of the coastal edge. Here too there was open ground, the sea on one side, the forest on the other, where settlements took advantage of a range of resources and potentials. Diverse wetland environments were also common on the southern fringes of the area, while in the east, the woodlands of many valleys rose up to meet more open country along the ridges of the limestone.[12]

> *I don't get up here, not in the summer . . . more when I was younger and first had the car . . . climbed a bit then . . . sometimes the clouds on the sea look like the fells . . . you forget which way you're looking . . . this time of year, there's no one here to speak of, it's not so bad . . .*

Scatters containing anything from a handful to several thousand pieces of worked flint and stone have been recovered in most of these areas. They occur along the coastal margin, from Walney Island, around St Bees, Drigg, Eskmeals and further to the north. Where conditions are good, these scatters sometimes contain the weathered bones of cattle, sheep, pigs and deer as well as the remains of shellfish. Mesolithic stonework is well represented in many, as are distinctive tools and waste from the Neolithic, including complete and broken stone axe blades.[13] These overlaps suggest that some places had long, if probably broken, sequences of occupation; histories that could be traced in the stone and in the condition and character of the cover. Paths from these settlements ran back inland along the sides of river valleys, carrying people over the wooded plain to higher ground and across the trails of others. Like the sea itself, many of these rivers were lines of movement and communication, identified in stories of other places and of origins. Lines to follow and to learn. Rivers and their terraces were also important to the east of the fells. Pollen and artefacts from the Eden Valley and adjacent limestone shelves also demonstrate a Mesolithic presence. What evidence there is suggests that clearance and settlement became more common in the area during the fourth millennium, small communities fastening upon or extending clearings and winding their way between them on both new and long established paths.

It is difficult to be certain when using this evidence. Woodlands are often altered by wildfires or by changes of fortune that have their own momentum. Breaks in cover open or close around fallen trees, stands die back and regenerate without assistance from people.[14] Things are never as uniform as they appear on modern plantations. Small groups could make use of clearings that opened without their help. They could also take a direct role, clearing ground with fire and axe, or through more patient practices like ring barking. Clearance served many purposes. Cut close to the earth, trees generated new shoots and an abundance of leaves that were easily reached and often favoured by browsing animals. The firing of woodland or scrub encouraged similar patterns of regeneration. This drew game along familiar paths, as well as providing fodder for stock.[15] The opening of the canopy was also a common precursor to settlement, the clearing of ground being one way that people made a commitment to particular places. In a country where unchecked woodland regeneration could have a significant impact in a handful of years, that commitment would need to be renewed. Clearance was often small scale but it was a familiar practice, the management of woodland a form of respect shown to country and to tradition. And with woodland management came the creation of resources to be harvested from one year or generation to the next. Coppicing generated browse. It also fostered the growth of underwood for hafts, or for rods to be woven into the fabric of buildings, baskets and hurdles.

There was a variety to the ways that people lived between and beyond the trees. Camps for a season or a handful of days, trails taken at certain times and places of more persistent occupation. Lodges behind the sand were visited from inland and sometimes by those who crossed the line where the sea met the sky. Many followed a seasonal round that carried them into different settings, established paths a reminder of those who had gone before. Some tasks were undertaken alone or with close kin, others in larger and more varied companies. A visit to an old hunting range, the pooling of labour in a clearing by the lake, collecting eggs or trapping birds on the beach. There were also times when people met by chance, or moved to join with others at a sacred site; a spring or prominent outcrop. Horizons were probably close in winter, snow and heavy seas discouraging major journeys. But when the land was born again, some remained while others moved; up in the hills, in a neighbouring valley or across the water. Some probably made even longer journeys. Life blurred around the edges.

> *. . . there was that time last year. Jesus he was lucky. We were running a training course with the big chainsaws and there was this one lad, quite experienced, who was set on a large ash. He knew his way around it but maybe his attention went, I don't know. Anyway, he'd got through the sapwood and when he hit the heart the blade kicked back, took a chunk off the side of his visor . . .he was grey and shaking for a good while after but he got the point . . . could've take his head off . . .*

Open canopied and light in places, dense and dark in others, woodlands were the familiar frame in which much of life unfolded. Places for food, for living and of spiritual importance, they carried the marks of a human and ancestral presence. They were crowded too; home to game and to animals that were feared or respected. Predators such as wolves, or the bears that seemed to live and move like people. Animals that lived in herds or solitary wanderers, it is likely that some species had a spiritual or metaphoric significance for people of the time. Trees themselves could also be understood in many ways. They set a pattern to activities and then, as now, were most likely a source of symbolism and identification. Different materials grew at different rhythms and needed different frequencies of attention. Coppice stools are often cut after the sap has fallen and understorey is best cleared out when dry. Toppled hardwoods may make the better fuel for fires, but they need to be cut before they harden. Tasks such as these may have been tied to the seasons and into longer cycles of movement and residence. Ring barking also demanded an acknowledgement of longer terms, a form of clearance that stretched over several years.

Where people did move from time to time, they did so in step with traditions that took them to places with a past. Their past and that of others. On a day-to-day basis and over the year, the condition of forests provided evidence of activity. A small group moving on a gathering trip recognised the subtle changes in the state of the ground that spoke of activity and the timescales

involved. In landscapes composed of small dispersed communities, these readings were important news to set alongside stories heard on the trail. The temporality of woodlands could also be acknowledged over longer timescales. With the passing of generations, the state of forests was a testament to the roots that linked people to the land. Located in oral tradition, the places where long dead kin once lived and worked could be recognised and remembered. Just as we can still recognise old coppice on the margins of Ruskin's estate at Brantwood, so people at the time were able to trace the mark of older phases of settlement and woodland management. Perhaps the clearings that opened of their own accord were seen this way, or even recognised as help given by the spirits who looked out for the living.

It was in these varied conditions that different communities began to involve themselves with stock and crops. Stock introduced a new thread to the rhythm of life. Like other creatures, they offered food to share and materials for clothing, tools and exchange. What made them different was that through accumulation, breeding and selection, they offered new ways of defining relations between people. Animals such as cattle or sheep were a source of wealth and standing and this was part of the reason they were adopted. The right to hold stock was probably a prerogative of particular age grades, the outlines of small herds often following ties of kinship. Involvement with stock also established new concerns, among them the requirement to bring cattle and sheep to seasonal pastures, and to keep them close in winter. Movement along the coast, between valleys and higher ground. Perhaps there were times when elders took children off to summer pastures, explaining the landmarks they encountered on the way. In the central fells, some of the earliest evidence that we have for this comes from around the Langdales. Pollen and charcoal beneath the peat in places like Langdale Coombe and Blea Tarn suggest that people exploited the high ground from an early stage. Whether this began as a way of guiding the browsing patterns of game we do not yet know, though this is certainly possible. But as stock became important, these grasslands took on a new significance as grazing, open country maintained by regular use and by periodic firing which kept the scrub at bay. It was no coincidence that there was also good stone in this area.

All these concerns involved dealing with others. Small groups were not entirely isolated and one of the hallmarks of the round was the movement and mingling of herds. Rustling saw animals move against the grain of relations and stock were traded or given as gifts to others. A calf delivered from close kin; a handful of animals married out across the ridge; a feast given in honour of visitors or the dead. For many communities, stock brought a twist in the content, if not the shape, of the annual cycle. They were also valued and it therefore mattered how animals fared. For people at the time, the changing fortunes of herds, the health of individual animals and success in breeding were a measure of practical experience. They were also an index against which to measure standing with the forces that watched over the living. The dead and other spirits had the power to help, to hinder or to turn their backs; they required respect. This weaving together of practical and social values meant that stock could be metaphors for the standing and composition of communities. Beyond the life cycle and the fortune of animals, there was the sense of bloodlines crossing and mingling when herds were brought close.

The first local experiments with crops may have begun on the coastal plain in the later Mesolithic. Beyond that, we know little about the spread or the character of cultivation. Some talk of gardens and of forest fallow on the coastal plain and lower slopes, cycles of planting and harvesting practiced only a handful of times. After the grazing of stubble, a patch was left to regenerate; scrub, then birch and ash; leaf litter and shadow. Soils depleted of fertility could be renewed in this way. Attention turned to other plots, last used a generation or more before, their presence still traceable in the composition of cover. Pasture perhaps, or open woods where boar rooted for fodder. For others, small fields were important in a different way. Sustained over longer periods, they provided fodder, materials and grain for food and drink. Stores to keep things going over winter; the makings of a feast to give to others. In such a physically varied region as Cumbria, we should not assume that the same routines were followed by every community. Diversity was an important dynamic in the trading that cut back and forth between families. Whatever the case, tensions could surround fields, just as they bordered pasture. As tenure shifted from one generation to another, new paths and new clearings could cut across old patterns and old agreements. If crops needed tending, so did the relationships that were worked into the land.

Like stock, crops required attention and they raised new concerns. They did not tie an entire community to one place for the whole year. But they needed to be maintained against the threat of deer or boar, while planting and harvesting required varied contributions of labour. They also added a new theme to thinking about land. Whatever the timing of cultivation, work was conducted by hand, not by the plough. This encouraged a tendency to choose lighter or sandier soils, near the coast or on the perched terraces that flanked the valleys on the limestone forelands. Crops also provided a rich source of metaphor and a concern with fortune. Where seasons changed the land in such a dramatic way, the sense of the world dying back and being reborn would have been nothing new. People had been harvesting the wild for generations and made sense of these cycles in customary ways. But crops engendered a particular form of involvement. This made their cycle of birth, death and rebirth a vivid metaphor for the lives of people and for the renewal and persistence of the community. Stock and crops also encouraged a different attitude towards time. In a world where the continuity of the line from one generation to another was a powerful concern, they were a debt owed to the past and a legacy to be bestowed on the future. Protection of that inheritance required

the passing on of practical knowledge. It also demanded a respect shown to those who held the fortunes of the living in their hands.

> *... the best method of chopping is one in which the blow is struck from the elbow, not the shoulder, with the axe meeting the tree at as acute an angle as possible. A long vertical flake should be detached at the outset; then as the notch in the tree gets more V-shaped, the flake to be struck will slope further and further in . . .*[16]

Life in Cumbria around five thousand years ago involved a tangle of relationships; with the land, with plants and animals and with other people. Stone axes were caught up in this tangle in many ways. In experienced hands, they helped people make spaces. Felling was not easy. A bad stance or the wrong angle would see the hard-won blade bounce off the trunk or even snap. You had to know your way around the task and around the timber itself. Was it seasoned, did it twist in tougher knots? There are many flakes from cutting edges which suggest that resharpening and reworking were a commonplace. And work did not begin and end with the crash of oak or elm. There was coppicing and shredding to produce leafy fodder for stock, the cutting back of scrub and understorey. On some blades, the angle of the cutting edge is tapered in from top to bottom. This is most likely a product of reworking over time, but is a form consistent with the sharp downward strokes associated with tasks like lopping. There was carpentry too; the patient splitting of planks, fencing, construction and sundry other tasks for which an axe, however hafted, was probably essential. Around the lodge or on the trail, an axe could be swung down from the shoulder for many reasons. And beyond wood there were other matters; animals to be slaughtered and butchered, ground to be turned, sometimes even people to fight – no shortage of uses for a well-balanced blade. These were skilful activities. It took time to learn how to work in particular ways, to find the path of least resistance through timber, to set a coppice stool, quarter a deer or make a haft. Familiarity with materials, like dexterity, had to be acquired – some tasks the prerogative of age and experience. Like stonework, it took time and practise to make the task look easy.

Axes meant many things, but their day-to-day importance in woodlands and around the lodge was part of the reason they were given other values. The routine need to maintain clearings or to create new pastures and plots brought the axe into close focus. It mattered that it was ready to hand and that was why it was so often to be found across the shoulder. And though things remained patchy, those needs increased with time and this gave an added importance to a good axe and good work. It was crucial to so much of life; an edge that could renew or transform the land around. It was crucial to fertility. In the changing conditions of the earlier fourth millennium, this helped to make the axe a potent and enduring symbol, something that carried you as much as it was carried.

A Cumbrian axe recovered from Etton, a Neolithic enclosure in the Fens. Brought back and carried along the extent of the hornstone.

Stickle Tarn – Harrison Stickle – Thorn Crag – Loft Crag – Pike of Stickle – Troughton Beck – Mart Crag – Langdale Combe – Black Crags – Pile of Stones – Rossett Pike – Cairns – Hard Crags – Flat Crags – Bowfell Links – Hart How – Sheepfold – Skilling Crag – Pen – Rough Crag – Mickledore – Pulpit Rock – Pikes Crag – Lingmell Coll – Piers Gill – Middleboot Knotts – Criscliff Knotts – Stand Crag – Spout Head – Great Slack – Cairn – Sprinkling Crags – Ruddy Gill – Allen Gill – Red Beck – Hind Side – Combe Head – Combe Door – Dovenest Crag

CHAPTER 4

POETRY IN AN UNKNOWN LANGUAGE

In much of his writing around and about Cumbria, Norman Nicholson tried to get under the skin of the land. For him, the rocks of the region were fundamental. They set a pattern, a potential for the shape and content of people's lives; how they lived and how they thought about themselves. Though the skin might change, the rock was at the base; a foundation of history and identity.[1]

Nicholson made various attempts to describe the shape and character of the region, particularly the radiating ridges and dales of the central massif. Wordsworth had re-used older descriptions to talk of two cartwheels, the western hub on Esk Hause, the eastern on Helvellyn. Others spoke of splayed hands back to back, the verdant tongues of the dales running up into the high ground like gaps between fingers. Nicholson saw a broken lemon squeezer, 'the dales gouged out of the dome and sloping radially to the rim'. And when it came to the ages of rocks, he saw an onion with its top sliced away; the older Skiddaw Slates and Borrowdale volcanics at the core, the younger limestones and sandstones the circles nearer the skin. There have been many other metaphors, parallels to catch the outcome of sedimentation and eruption, of uplift, faulting and the slow grind of ice. Most rely upon a certain point of view, one gained by a hard climb or the privileged elevation of a map. Most fail.

Robert Hills. Slate Quarry, Langdale. Birmingham City Museum and Art Gallery

Nicholson himself acknowledged this failure, and that may be why his focus was often tighter. His grand view was usually a preamble to more detailed observations on the ground; ice scratches on a fellside, sulky hummocks or a blunt-headed mountain bullocking into the green. It may also explain his interest in the invitations that the rock extended to people. The coal that ran out from the coast beneath the youngest sand and clay, the sandstones carved for red buildings in the north and west, the copper above Coniston. The chance of a dual economy, or an industry around which towns could coalesce. Farmers working stone in the slack times of the agricultural calendar; whole communities tying their fortunes to extraction. Above all else were the Borrowdale volcanics. Lava, ash and dust spewed out from submarine volcanoes which settled on the Skiddaw Slate. Altered by pressure and buckled by uplift, the series contains stone of many qualities, each with its own name: Scafell Ash, Honister Slate, Esk Pike Hornstone, Shap Rhyolite. A variety in structure and toughness that influenced the course of glaciers and determined the shape of fells and dales. Steep lava cliffs and more gentle and abraded ashy slopes; fractured blockfields and scree. Here too was potential, recognised in the scars of mines and quarries, where roofing slate, building stone or other minerals had been won.

> *. . . To look at the scenery without trying to understand the rock is like listening to poetry in an unknown language . . .*

There are many histories of mining and quarrying in Cumbria. Often local and intimate, the accent in most accounts inclines towards a human scale; how stone and ore defined communities.[2] But most quarries were also part of broader worlds, recognised in sales and other contract documents, in the roll call of leaseholders and the changing names of companies. In Borrowdale, mining for copper and for lead was established by the Company of Mines Royal in the sixteenth century, deep bites around Newlands and Dalehead. Skilled miners from Germany and Holland came and settled in some numbers, their presence traceable in parish registers and in the local terms that are sometimes used for different aspects of the work. Copper was being extracted around Coniston even earlier, the village sustained by the mineral and the slate. On Seatoller Fell, where the blackened tongues of graphite spoil can still be traced, 'wad' was being extracted by the early sixteenth century and perhaps even before that, work suspended every so often to keep the value high.[3] At Honister and Yew Crags, where the wind is sometimes 'so strong you can see it', work began on the surface at around the same time, massive slates picked over and split by men who lived rough on the fellsides during the working week. Seasonal at first and always at risk from the weather, the working of the 'slate metal' became more consistent, extending underground as demand increased. And as demand rose, so did rents; the annual sum paid to Lord

The Langdales

Leconsfield rising from two pounds in 1728 to two hundred and fifty pounds a century later.[4]

Work at many mines and quarries changed with urban and industrial expansion at the very time that the Lakes were becoming valued as classic ground. Some even became the subjects of the new way of seeing. Demanded by a market that was both local and worldwide in its extent, the graphite above Seathwaite was so valuable that the miners who walked miles to work were sometimes strip-searched, guards keeping watch to prevent theft and espionage. Yet the wad mines were also a noted tourist attraction, visited early on by Thomas Gray and since then by many others. The area was a wonder, not just because of the wealth that lay beneath the fellside, nor simply for the dark and dramatic character of the work itself. It was the setting, perched high above a narrow and introverted dale, with darker fells towering up on most sides and the cascade of Sour Milk Ghyll. For those in search of the Sublime, there was much to wonder at. As John Dalton put it in his 'descriptive poem' of 1755: 'Horrors like these at first alarm,/ But soon with savage grandeur/ charm/ And raise to noblest thought the/ mind . . .'.

Three ways of seeing side by side. Appetites for the view and for the wealth that could be cut from the rock; a closer focus born out of labour. As demand grew, leases became the subject of intense competition, new owners introducing blasting and mechanisation to increase production.[5] What had often

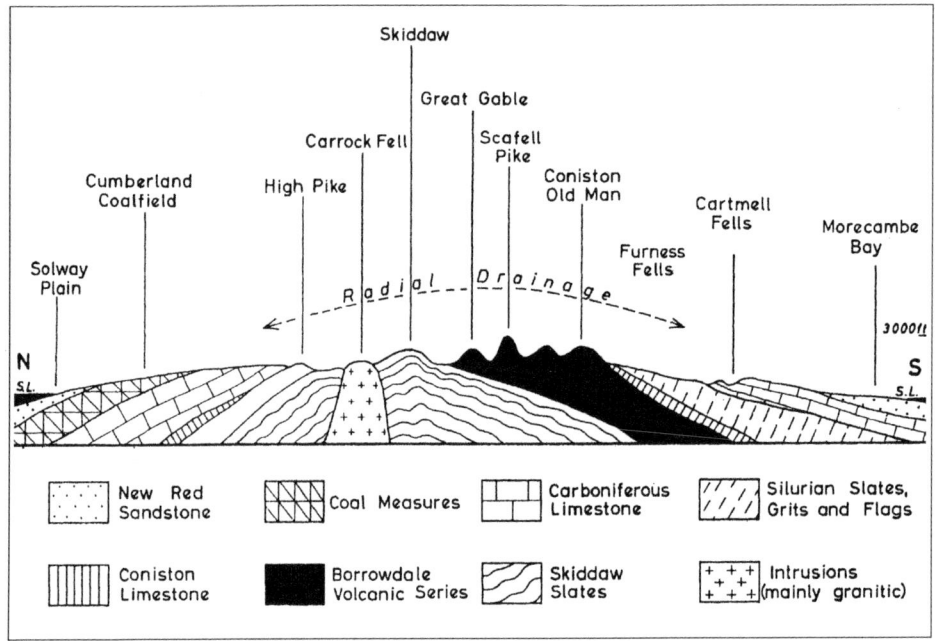

A simplified north–south section through the principal geology of Cumbria

The Langdales

Worked slate above Chapel Stile

begun as a seasonal venture became more continuous employment. Tools, skills and stone broke up between people in more definite chains of operation. Extraction, docking, riving and dressing; mining, crushing, washing and smelting. Work became a living, encouraging settlement in nearby towns and villages, close attachment recognised in the stone used for building and in payrolls from one generation to the next. Crags became familiar, acquiring local histories. How work often meant separation from the family for days and how the dust of dry stone ate into the chest. Stories connected to people in ways that geological terms do not, memory rather than memoir.[6]

> . . . *John Rigg lived in Chapel Stile and worked at Newton Quarry from 1880 to 1901. He walked to work each day, three miles there and back again. Twenty one years. Thirty eight thousand, three hundred and ninety miles give or take a few . . .*

Quarrying around the Langdales has been no less varied. Borrow pits and shallow scoops mimic the lines of several walls; dips and hollows made as farmers took rock that was ready to hand for a local boundary. Split slates in the southern half of the valley, beck cobbles in the north, the immediacy of need reflected in the parallel. Older walls themselves could serve as sources, dismantled to create new and more extensive holdings or to maintain collective features. Ties to land and to the more dispersed community of the valley. For those who lived close, the style of the build could reveal particular hands. Houses also made demands upon the fells, and it is not uncommon to find quarry scoops near many, their sharp edges lost beneath a mantle of turf.

More specific sources can also be traced; stone for buildings and for other purposes. Above Robinson Place for example, stone was cut at faces on either side of the intake boundary, a sledway carrying slates downslope for dressing. Haematite was mined in the area during the seventeenth and eighteenth centuries, leaving covered shafts and spoil heaps at several locations. In an essay on the natural history of the region from 1709, Robinson noted that the '. . . Langdale and Cunningston mountains do abound most with Iron veins; which supplies with ore and keeps constantly going, a furnace at Langdale; where great plenty of good and malleable iron is made . . .'.[7] Mines were dug at Bowfell, Ore Gap, Browney Gill and Red Tarn, material carried out by Browney and Wrynose Gills and down the zigzag sledway that descends by Rossett Gill, a route now used as a tourist path. The furnace noted by Robinson is now untraceable, though material was also being worked at Hackett Forge in Little Langdale and in Langstrath to the north. We know little of how work was organised, whether it was full time, or scheduled into the agricultural year as part of a dual economy. This was not uncommon in the region at that time, though Robinson's comments suggest that work was more persistent; people binding their lives more completely to the ore. Hands and

Thrang Crag slate quarry, Great Langdale. Thomas Allom 1833. Kendal Library

The Langdales

faces reddened by the work, some were drawn from families who kept farms in the dales below.

There are larger quarries too, the stone supporting the growth of villages at Elterwater and Chapel Stile. Places like Thrang Crag, Colt Howe, Spout Crag, Bank and Lingmoor, that hang above Little Langdale. A hard stone that takes a good polish, the grey-green slates of the area have long been prized for buildings, headstones and other decorative pieces. The market remains extensive. Beyond local graveyards, buildings and gift shops, Langdale slate is prominent on buildings in Glasgow, London, Copehagen, Dallas and Hong Kong. By the nineteenth century, this demand was being met by an industry that spread across many fellsides, providing income, a pattern to life and an affront to the sensibilities of at least some visitors. Charges were provided from the gunpowder works at Elterwater which employed over eighty men itself and sent a number to a premature rest in the churchyard in Chapel Stile. Between one and two hundred people worked the stone of the valley each day, drilling, hammering, sawing and splitting slatemetal to be carted out beyond Skelwith Bridge. The same paths up and down, horses, sledges and stone. Blasting and rock falls, the sound of machinery and of working by hand. Echoes can be heard around Elterwater and Skelwith, where stone is still worked.

Most quarries have long since fallen silent. Scattered along the fellsides, the screes that spill down from old faces are spattered with the browns and greens

Sawing slate at Moss Rigg Quarry, Elterwater. Photo: Geoffrey Berry

Walling source and cleared stone above Pye Howe

of moss. Easily missed until the sun hits the stone after the rain, most lie on tracks that have not been beaten for years. And though most have names that are locally familiar, the majority appear on maps as generic places – their presence marked by paths that seem to go nowhere, or simply by 'Quarry (dis)' or 'Quarries (disused)'.[8] Visiting Langdale today, it is already difficult to get a sense of the scale and character of stone extraction over the last two centuries. How the biographies of crags and people overlapped for local reasons and sometimes because of more distant demands. Things were no less intimate in the Neolithic. Even then, there was a loose articulation between the local and the distant. But the world itself was different. For many communities of the time, the high volcanics lay not at the heart but on the edge of things, the world beyond them a subject of stories and not of economic certainties. The stone was different too, its origins and associations spoken of in a language that is lost to us. Finding a way in is no mean task.

> . . . *all jobs have a number, but you know mostly where it's going . . . sometimes on holiday or down south, I'll see the front of a building and know the stone . . . but the big stuff goes abroad . . .*

Split slate steps and working debris, Chapel Stile

In Cumbria, as in other regions, there were many ways that people got hold of stone, some traditions stretching back into the Mesolithic. Material could be acquired by chance; good stone stumbled upon where storms had toppled timber or separated sand and shingle on the 'highest rung' of the tide. There was trade with others met on the trail and perhaps with partners who were distant kin. Stone was also won through visits to long established sources, on a beach or in the sides of a familiar river. Much of this was flint; nodules scooped up by the ice, abraded into cobbles and pebbles and dumped with the clays along the coast. The cortex or rind of these pieces is often rounded and weathered, a contrast to the fresher mottled stone within. Grey and darker cherts could also be found within some of the limestones. A rock with similar properties to flint, it could be prized from the grasp of its yellow-white parent and flaked into many forms. A blade to be used as it was – a scraper, knife or arrowhead; a core to carry on the trail in anticipation of need. Scatters containing these materials are common and extensive along the coastal margin and on the limestone shelves above the Eden Valley. Tools and waste from episodes of occupation stretching between the Mesolithic and the Bronze Age.

In a region where good stone was not available everywhere, where the seasons carried some to different places, it mattered to pay the stone respect through careful working. That may be why many of the cores and tools that we find are small, extensively worked or exhausted. Such careful working took time to learn. Hands did not become accustomed overnight and because of this, skill was an index of progression in life, one expression of the journey that carried a child towards adulthood.

Found in a sandhill or in a scatter across a field, tools and flakes of flint and chert are difficult to source. We often cannot say with confidence where the stone originated. That was probably not the case in the Neolithic. Communities of the time were far more accomplished at reading this material, tracing in the mottling of flint or the colour of the chert the location and associations of certain sources or areas. Even different ways of working said something about the identities of people who left broken stone on the trail. To grow up on the coastal plain or the limestone fringes was to become skilful in reading these signs. It meant learning the lie of the land, its seasonal rhythms and its history. Where could good material be found? What were the best times for collecting stone eggs from the beach, where did flint getting require consultation with others? Some deposits had been used for generations and were probably visited by people drawn from different lines. They were places where others might be met from time to time, a chance to exchange and renew connections. Use entailed customary rights of access which were as much about ties between people as they were about the stone.

Use also meant respect paid to tradition, an act which helped to renew a sense of tenure with the land. Moving with stock or harvesting the forest, the younger members of a community learnt how to recognise material just as they

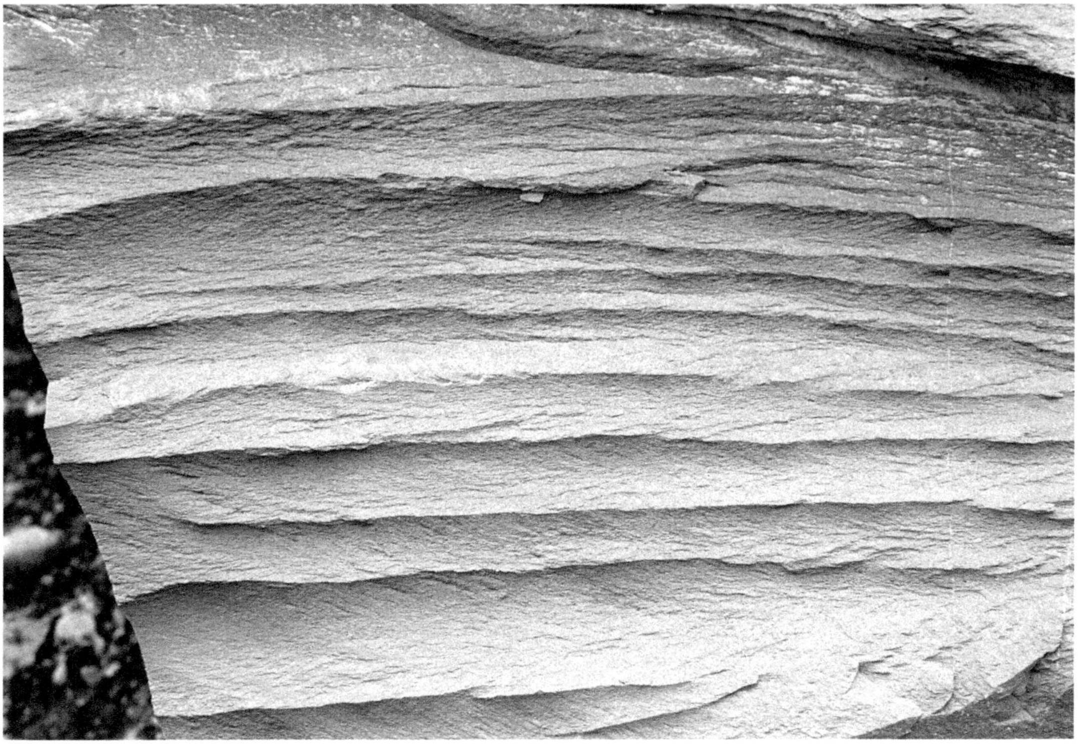

Poetry in an Unknown Language

learnt how to work it. Checking the soil grasped in the roots of an upturned tree, following cobbles in a river or scouring the beach after a storm.[9] And observation or instruction went hand in hand with other things; with the telling of stories about the land and the past, how ties with others were caught up in the act. Perhaps there were even stories about the origins of the stone itself.

Not all material came so readily and directly to hand. The evidence is fragmented and partial at best, but there are stones that speak of different journeys. Near the coast, assemblages eroding from sand dunes and raised beaches sometimes include flakes of flint that came from the other side of the Irish Sea. There are also distinctive tools, scrapers or arrowheads with hollow bases which are more familiar in the inventories of excavations in Ireland or on the Isle of Man. In the south and east, scatters sometimes include flint likely to have originated over the Pennines in Yorkshire, and there is at least one porcellanite axe in the area from Tievebulliagh, County Antrim. An ebb and flow across the water or through the hills, the movement back and forth of people, materials and ideas.

These were the patterns of stone choice and use that had characterised life in and around the region for centuries, perhaps for millennia. Invitations offered by the land or by others, taken up by people whose lives wound between two coasts and towards the fells, or from the Eden valley to the foothills of the Pennines. Some of these patterns persisted throughout prehistory. But by what

The Langdales

we measure as the fourth millennium, new choices were being made; journeys to the higher fells and the getting of stone that lent itself to axe making.

> . . . these implements occur most frequently in the northern part of Britain, especially in Cumberland and Westmorland, in consequence, it may be supposed, of the felspathic rocks, of which they are usually formed, being there found in the greatest abundance . . . [10]

We can date with some accuracy when the source became a focus of archaeological attention. Reports of axes have a long pedigree, stretching back across the nineteenth century and in sufficient detail for Sir John Evans to be able to talk in the 1870s about the regional abundance of the stone from which many were made. However, it took quite a while before a specific provenance became clearer. Discussion of outcrops and flaking floors on the fells start to appear in the archaeological literature in the first few decades of the twentieth century, the result of observations by Watson, Plint and others.[11] Interest gathered pace, collections grew, and what was first referred to as the 'Stake Pass Industry' was re-named by Clare Fell to reflect a more substantive link with Great Langdale. By the 1940s, discussion of evidence from the Langdales went hand in hand with the detailed characterisation of axe and adze blades that had wandered far beyond the region.[12] Work on both these fronts has continued ever since. Because of this, we know that the volcanics and adjacent rocks of the central fells offered a good deal to prehistoric communities. Some were weak and laminar and ill-suited for working.

Others could be pecked and ground into shape, the debris of working no more than dust and small chips. But a few, like the volcanic tuffs around the Langdales, bore at least one striking resemblance to flint. They could be flaked systematically, their fine-grained structure allowing the force from a blow to travel smoothly through the stone. They could then be ground to a fine finish.

We also know that working happened not at one specific place but across a fairly broad area. A range of outcrops were recognised and worked to varying degrees, so much so that petrologists are still uncertain as to just how many different places were exploited.[13] The rock also varies within particular outcrops, making characterisation all the more difficult.[14] As if this was not enough, some stone was found away from its source; carried as an erratic in the underbelly of the ice and worked where it was deposited when temperatures rose. At present it is best to say that the range of stones and the number of axes worked in the central fells may well have been underestimated.

One particular outcrop was heavily favoured in prehistory, a band of fine grained stone that occurs between the 500- and 900-metre contours within what are known as the Seathwaite Fell Tuffs. Originally described as '. . . an epidotised tuff of intermediate or basic composition . . .', it is thankfully also known by some as hornstone. This hard volcanic ash lies bedded between coarser tuffs, rising and falling as it makes its sinuous journey through the fells. The outcrop runs for some 19 kilometres from Stickle Tarn, taking in the northern side of the Langdale valley before heading south and west behind Bow Fell, to curl around Scafell Pike. From there it heads north-east, behind Great End and Sprinkling Tarn, running out beyond Glaramara. Such a deceptively simple description and entirely historical. A consequence of geology, a discipline that settled into shape around the time of the Romantics, it also strings together names that have longer roots. Some are Old Norse, referring to topography and to pastoral shelters, others to people or industry, none of them as old as the Neolithic.[15]

The hornstone presents itself in forms which influenced the manner and extent of prehistoric working. In places, it is heavily fractured and resists the hammer, shattering rather than flaking when a blow is struck. In others, the stone presents no such problems and takes the hammer well. Not all outcrops with these potentials show signs of working, but there are many that do. Scars on the face, scatters of flakes and shattered stone. Scraped by the ice, the hornstone occurs in impressive near vertical crags. Benches, embayments and overhangs occur where joints and minor faults created paths of least resistance for water and ice. Such conditions are common around the Langdales. In other places, faults were more aggressively attacked by the elements, splitting the stone and creating blockfields, weathered and angular surfaces concealing the finer blue-green stone within. These are found around the Langdales and are typical of the conditions found across Scafell Pike and Glaramara. Stone is also

Scafell and Mickledore. Photo: Armitt Library

Loft Crag, looking east. Photo: Geoffrey Berry

found in numerous screes, where weathered scabs of frost cracked rock lie mingled with the debris of working. Easily set in motion by water, feet and hooves, some screes lie hundreds of feet below the outcrop and were themselves a source of workable material. The most dramatic of these, South Scree, is a long tongue of eroded stone that has flowed down to the Mickleden Valley between Middle Gully and the Pike of Stickle.[16]

Sadly, we cannot trace the origins of the source in anything like the same detail. We do not know when the stone was first identified and worked, nor how it was characterised and named. Where we see one raw material, people at the time may have classified the stone according to many criteria. Colour, texture and extent, history, spiritual associations or the time and company of the approach. Few of our certainties may have mattered. Flakes of a fine grained tuff appear in some Mesolithic scatters in the lowlands and these hint at a knowledge of the stone and its location long before the Neolithic. However, these are often the result of flaking pebbles transported to lower ground by the ice and the working of these erratics probably continued into the Neolithic. Hunters and gatherers of earlier generations certainly followed trails that took them into the fells. A periodic presence where the forest edge met the higher, open country, the taking of game and a seasonal encounter with others. It may have been in this sort of setting that the outcrop itself was identified, though there is as yet no clear evidence that it was the stone that drew them up. For the moment, all we have to go on are radiocarbon dates and associations for axes found in Cumbria and elsewhere. These all suggest that journeys to extract and work the stone only became significant around the start of the fourth millennium. If there was working before that, it was directed towards other ends and scratched no more than the surface.

How did people find the rock? Given the patterns of life followed by earlier generations, the lie of the land around the Langdales was probably familiar, at least to some. There were named places and paths long before the stone was fastened upon. Against that background, material may have been followed up streams and becks, distinctive cobbles traced back towards their source, growing more abundant with proximity. Just why people started to make the journey is less clear. Though there was some variety to be found in Cumbria, most deposits of flint and chert could only deliver small nodules and tablets. These could be worked in many ways, but were often too small to make larger tools such as axes. Not so up in the fells, where there was literally a mountain of material. But why then? What had changed to prompt the climb? The worn and battered cutting edges of many blades is evidence enough of a practical demand. But there was more to it than that. An idea that travelled between regions in the form of a blade, in words spoken on the trail or at seasonal gatherings. The utility of axes had been established long before. By the earlier Neolithic, it was their importance as tokens of identity that encouraged the climb.

The Langdales

TRANCE AND DELIGHT

It may have been these qualities that lay behind the working of specific outcrops, not least the distinctive peaks of the Langdales which even at a distance, tend to catch the eye. Good stone could be had elsewhere, some of it more easily reached whichever direction one came from. What mattered were the distance and the climb, to places only seen on the horizon when the trail brought them into view. To crags that were dangerous and sometimes unstable, that could vanish in the cloud and lead you on false trails in harsh conditions. A place of fractured stone where a wrong step could be your last, where only the swifts move in and out with ease.

> *... I passed down from Broadcrag, skirted the precipices, and found myself cut off from a most sublime Crag-summit, that seemed to rival Sca'Fell Man in height, and to outdo it in fierceness ... The first place I came to that was not direct Rock, I slipped down and went on for a while with tolerable ease – but now I came (it was midway down) to a smooth perpendicular rock about 7 feet high – this was nothing – I put my hands on the ledge, and dropped down. In a few yards came just such another. I dropped that too. And yet another, seemed not higher – I would not stand for a trifle, so I dropped that too – but the stretching of the muscle of my hands and arms, and the jolt of the Fall on my Feet, put my whole Limbs in a Tremble, and I paused, and looking down, saw that I had little else to encounter but a succession of these little Precipices – it was in truth a Path that in very hard Rain is, no doubt, the channel of a most splendid waterfall. So I began to suspect that I ought not to go on; but then unfortunately, though I could with ease drop down a smooth Rock of 7 feet high, I could not climb it, so go on I must; and on I went. The next three drops were not half a Foot, at least not a foot, more than my own height, but every Drop increased the palsy of my Limbs. I shook all over, Heaven knows without the least influence of Fear, and now I had only two more to drop down – to return was impossible – but of these two the first was tremendous. It was twice my own height, and the Ledge at the bottom was exceedingly narrow, that if I dropt down upon it I must of necessity have fallen backwards and of course killed myself. My limbs were all in a tremble – I lay upon my back to rest myself, and was beginning according to my Custom to laugh at myself for a Madman, when the sight of the Crags above me on each side, and the impetuous Clouds just over them, posting so luridly and rapidly northward, overawed me. I lay in a state of almost prophetic Trance and Delight ...*

Coleridge's account of his headlong scramble down Broad Stand conveys the immediacy and elation associated with the Romantic cult of the mountains.[17] And though it is a descent that he describes, it anticipates something of the

buzz derived from going the other way; the intense experience and focus of those who began to climb in earnest in the fells towards the end of the nineteenth century. Time experienced in snatches; the loss of self and shifts of scale. Interest in the journey as much as the summit. Coleridge's mad dash downhill is important. It reminds us that whatever Ruskin may have argued about the primacy of vision, there are many qualities to the understanding of an area like Langdale that we simply cannot take from an image. Qualities that are experienced through the body rather than the eye. It also raises a problem. In arguing that the crags were dramatic and challenging even in the Neolithic, are we simply extending back a view that is itself historical – a product of conditions no more than a couple of centuries old?

Perhaps a little. Living with the legacy of those traditions, it is difficult to avoid entirely. But the argument does not rest there. Long before Thomas Gray delighted in his terror, before Ruskin reconciled the creation with the living geology of Coniston Old Man, there were pilgrims climbing holy mountains. A tradition traced most powerfully to the fourth century and the hermit Saint Jerome, high places were the epitome of wilderness and ascetic rigour. Vision was possible for those who had freed themselves from worldly care by their withdrawal uphill. In the late medieval world, peaks also took you close to the divine, the climb a metaphor used by Dante, Petrarch and other writers to describe the scramble towards revelation and redemption. The harder and more perilous the scramble, the greater the deliverance. The prospect offered by elevation could also be a basis for authority, or at least for a claim. The peaks on many early pilgrimage routes had other names long before their association with particular saints. So did the distant mountains that Victorian explorers 'conquered' later on, ascent and renaming a part of the colonial process. Even now, whether you say 'Snowdon' or '*Yr Wyddfa*' depends very much upon your sense of history and identity.

A divine association with high ground can also be traced in classical sources and in the ritual sanctuaries that people carved into crags at the time. Places where help might be sought and sanction given, respect shown through both the climb and through offerings. In the traditions of the Tao in China, sacred mountains also connected heaven and earth. Holding the celestial realm aloft, they were the abode of the immortals, a retreat for only the purest of shamans where a sort of epiphany could be had, the body losing its substance to the air. Similar themes can be traced in the shamanic traditions of Central Asia and Northern Europe. A veneration of remote, high places where transformation was possible; a tendency to trace the shape of a spirit in the form of particular outcrops. Mountains also loom large in origin myths, in stories that connect people to the land and to each other through the past. Many of the peaks of North America were named, respected and prominent in oral tradition long before Plymouth Rock. A result of the actions of transforming spirits, they were a focus for tribal identities and a context for rites of passage. Slopes upon

Poetry in an Unknown Language

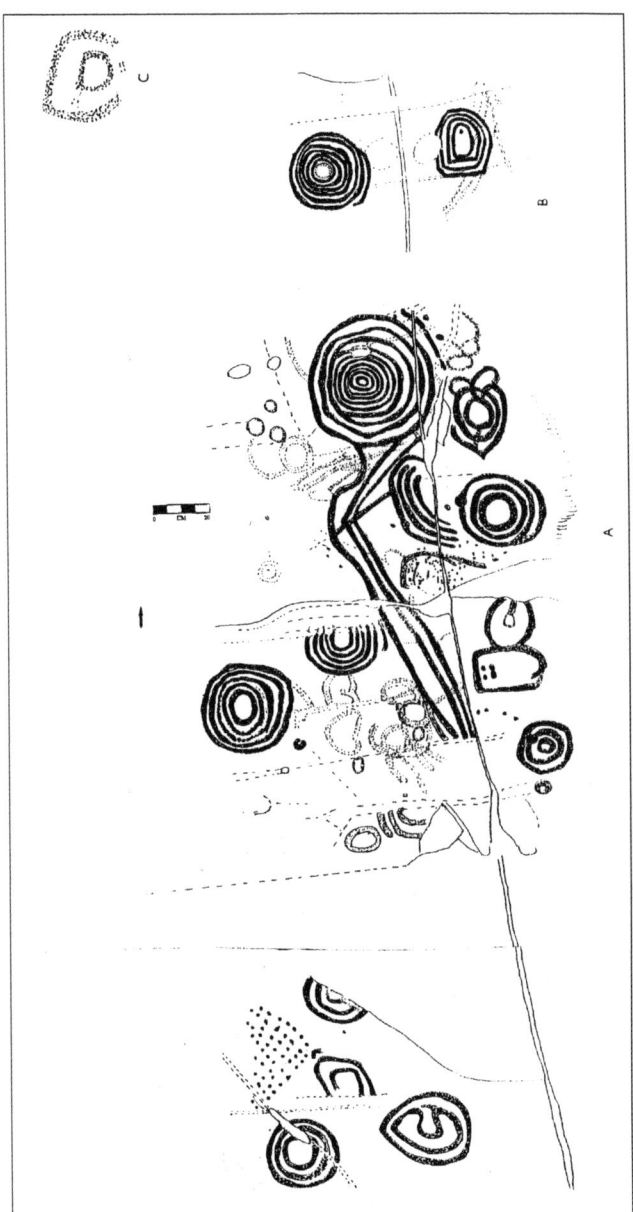

Rock carvings at Copt Howe.
Copyright Beckensall, 2002

which to hunt and loftier retreats where visions were received by a shaman or by those crossing the threshold into adulthood. It was only much later that they were recast as 'wilderness' to suit the origin myths of the new nation state. A similar sequence can be traced in Arnhem Land. Aboriginal 'Dreamtime' accounts discern the actions of ancestral beings in prominent outcrops, places of observance and, at times, of ritual gatherings. Some mark where a spirit being was drawn into the earth. Some are even the remains of the ancestors themselves; their bones, their blood, their semen. And some are also quarries.

The stories and the spirits in the stone lend a powerful quality to tools that are made by the right people at the right time.

Elevated places have been prominent in the imaginations of many cultural traditions, in part because they impose themselves so powerfully upon the senses. What they have meant has been specific to time and place. But against this background, to suggest that those who scrambled up the Cumbrian fells in the Neolithic did so only in a detached and utilitarian manner is to impose a yet more recent conceit upon the past. For people who spent a good deal of their time a few days' walk away, a visit to the source involved a journey. It carried them away from more familiar ranges and from at least some of the familiar community. It brought them into contact with crags that demanded the gift of their energy and perhaps other gifts besides. The way could be dangerous, work was hard and stone would not be won without some form of observance.

These journeys were often made with stock. Though the treeline in the central fells was up near the crags, pollen and charcoal from places like Langdale Coombe suggest that regular grazing and even periodic firing discouraged regeneration from an early stage. By using the land in this way, people kept it open, a small scale anticipation of more recent and extensive grazing. Tending to country renewed a connection with an area that gave stone as well as pasture to help stock through the bite of the winter. There were, of course, other places where animals could be fattened before the land died back. What the Langdales offered was a time and place apart where other interests were also served. As some watched stock from temporary camps, others attended to the outcrop, getting the stone from which roughouts could be fashioned. Given the setting and the sharpness of changes in the fells, this was a periodic event, perhaps seasonal. There is no evidence to suggest permanent occupation at these elevations, nor in the dales immediately below. When the time was right, people took to the trail with their herds, the smoke from their lodges dwindling in the distance behind them. Up the sides of river valleys, through dense and tangled dales and along more open ridges, they camped along the way, revisiting clearings or forest edges where old hearths could still be traced. Every once in a while, the pikes swung into view above the forest. Two or three days, maybe more; there were always other matters to attend to. And at the end of the trail, the sharpening of breath, a steeper climb to old camps near the head of the beck. Fires lit and preparations made amidst the scattered flakes of earlier work. A glance along the fellside where other fires were already burning.

Where the goal of working was to make tools which said something about you, the journey and a measure of separation conferred a special quality to both the act and the artefact. These are the hallmarks of many rites of passage; conventions that mark the crossing of important thresholds in life. The reaching of a certain age gave younger members of a line the right to make the journey

Harry Place bouldering. Photo: Nick Wharton

with older and more senior kin. Where that happened, the trail was also a path for a narrative, an account of origins, of how the histories of people and land could be read. Places on the way that had genealogical or ancestral connections, signs of earlier journeys and even sites held as sacred.

Just such a place may have been recognised at Copt Howe, near Harry Place, where a massive boulder has been carved with cup marks, concentric circles and other lines. Others probably lie as yet unrecognised on different approaches to the crags. Some say that the images are effectively a map of the fells, the stone sitting at a point on the approach where the crags can be seen on the horizon. Used now by climbers practising their bouldering skills, the carvings on the rock are undated and open to several interpretations. Like other carvings in the region, some of them may belong to the Neolithic. People probably paused here, renewed their tenure with the area through the payment of respect and passed on secrets to those who had not been this way before. No doubt there were other places too, many that we now overlook as 'natural'. That said, rumours circulate, as they often do, that the carvings are no more than a century old, many of them carved by a Victorian or later hoaxer. When so many museum archives contain 'Neolithic' axes of an equally recent date, these claims have to be taken seriously. Here at least, it is probably best to say that we simply do not know just how old all the carvings are.[18] What we can say with more confidence is that for those making the journey for the first time, the walk in brought new knowledge just as it broadened horizons. And at the end of the trail was the stone. Grey-green, distinctive and easily recognised. Spirits willing, there were good blades to be had if one knew how to work it right.

What people saw as they climbed and scrambled towards the source is, in the strict sense, impossible to reconstruct. A delightful horror; a holy terror? Probably not. In the landscapes of the time, the outcrops were regarded in ways that crossed the lines we draw between history, geology and myth. They still do; valued by some for their offer of extremity, of revelation and renewal, a hurdle to others in search of lost stock, *terra incognita* when the cloud comes down. For those who lived long before the certainties of the Romantic vision, perhaps the crags were even then tied to a sense of the spiritual. A legacy of the ancestors or their remains; the memory of earlier generations tied to individual crags and floors. Perhaps there were even spirits in the clouds, their presence heard in the echoes that bounced around the work. There is no reason to assume that though working was hard, it was simply instrumental, hammers brought down on inert material. This was a powerful place, as prominent in the imagination as it was on the skyline. The approach was bound with proscriptions, gifts required before the crags gave up their own.

DORRY

27 March 1932
Just arrived here and it's pouring! But the country and scenery is splendid. Jenny's wedding went off very well. Her people came after all and several college folk. Alice was there. More news later. Love to all. Dorothy

For Dorothy Curtis, a lifelong attachment to the Lakes began in the early 1920s; family legend has it that she was YHA member number thirty-seven. Though that number is only an estimate, she was there from an early stage and was walking familiar fells when ramblers began to organise and trespass.

30 March 1932
Win and I have abandoned the Four and are staying with Dot Shaw's sister in Ulverston and doing the Lakes from there. Had a marvellous tour yesterday – Coniston and Hawkshead ending here in Windermere for the night – today, after a marvellous walk, rain all the way, went from Langdale to Borrowdale and then Keswick. Love to all. Dot. ps. please preserve the card

After graduation, she worked as a teacher where that attachment was soon shared by members of the 'Discoverers' walking club that she helped to run. Many girls followed in her footsteps, maintaining what they shared through postcards for the rest of their lives.

1 September 1934
Just had lunch up by these glorious tarns and the girls have been swimming. It's just lovely to be here again. We've had good weather so far. Today is glorious. Yesterday saw Grasmere & surroundings & in all walked 20 miles. Love Dorothy

On 10 August 1935 she married Jack Wheeler, but the rambling and scrambling continued. Beyond the more rigid confines of the school, there was a chance of relationships which were personal rather than professional.

15 September 1937
Dear Mrs Wheeler. At last Jean and I have managed to get to the lakes and now our ambition is realised. We are both having a spiffing time! We are sleeping together so we just talk for ages and go throughly mad. Anyway, please don't tell Miss Smith because she seems to think that I am too young! Love from Joan. ps. I think I've seen a very good example of a 'u' shaped valley! Anyway, I hope I'm right.

Sometimes it was altogether more private, a walk along the same path.

18 August 1939
Had a grand week in the lakes – glorious weather as usual. Dragged Jack up the traverse of Great Gable – it was grand. Stayed near Crummock and Loweswater. Saw Hawes-water, in process of being submerged & the dam is half finished & all buildings, including this church pulled down. Love to you both. Cheerio. D & J. ps. Can I have the card back later

In the end, it was common ground, a chance of renewal and the possibility of new connections. Like many women of her generation, rambling for Dorry was as social as it was personal, an act of renewal and reunion, an attitude that bled into the political.

4 September 1954
We've reached my favourite spot at last. The weather is holding well and we've done no end of good climbing. We climbed Scafell Pikes today and came down this pass shown on this card. We are going up this mountain – Great Gable – tomorrow. All feeling very very fit. Hope you are too. My love as ever. Dorothy

Dorothy's ashes were scattered on Great Gable on 31 May 1997

CHAPTER 5

TENURE

The Romantic gaze involved a close attention to the lakes and fells. Visitors made journeys further west to visit ruinous antiquities and others of their kind, often travelling along the turnpike roads that were being built around that time. But their gaze was resolutely fastened on the Lake District, a part of the region that has ever since been mistaken for the whole. Just as the Claude glass tinted a scene with the shades of a selected season, so the filter of the Romantics screened out the complexities of rural life; the threads that ran beyond the classic ground.[1] Though some struggled to find a poetic equivalence with the sower or the shepherd, most were content with an image of a close-grained pastoral existence that left out the politics of past and present.

Not everyone bought the myth, even at the time – mainly those who treated the Lakes as a 'Butlin camp of the sensibilities'.[2] But the appetite for sentimental visions of the area remained considerable.[3] If anything, it increased as the range and number of visitors was swelled by the railways in the mid-nineteenth century, a development protested against by Wordsworth and later by Ruskin.[4] By then, the emphasis and the audience had shifted, the central lakes important to the urban middle classes for the contrast that they offered to the more mechanical qualities of urban and industrial life.[5]

What many visitors continued to miss were the broader connections. The routes they took were not maintained simply for their convenience. They carried people and materials and had done so long before the sublime fells were drawn from rough and uninviting country. Stock and wool to various markets; stone and charcoal, timber and ore to the towns and ports along the coast.

Ringarth and intake walls picked out in light snow below the Pikes. Photo: Geoffrey Berry

Cairns beyond the enclosed land, Mickleden

Tenure

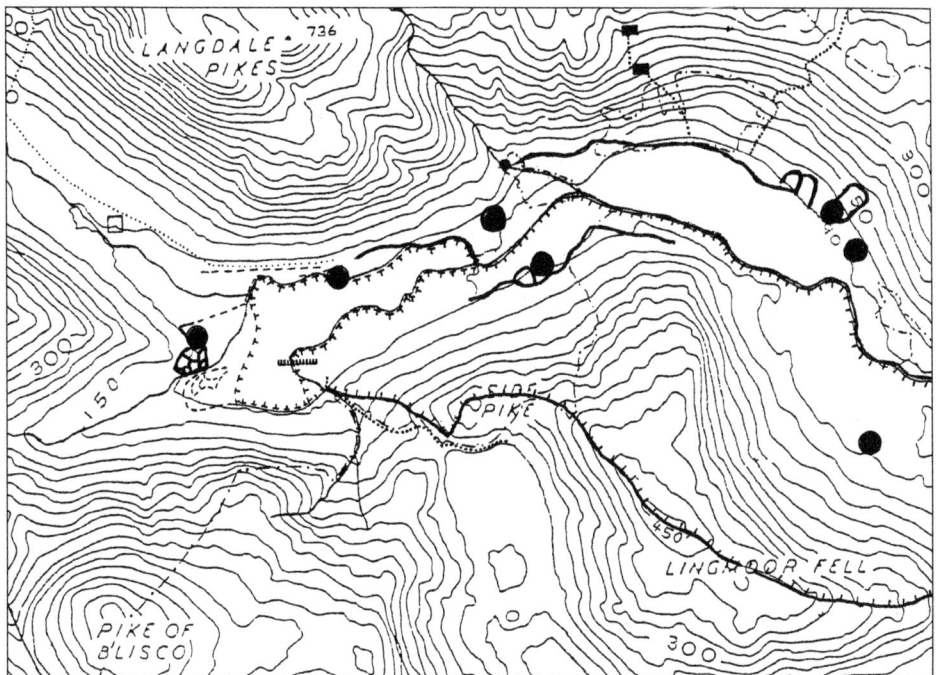

Enclosure was limited at first; a few farms and shielings and the ringarth, the line of the manor boundary walled over Lingmoor and following the water in the dale. Source: National Trust

When West published his guide in 1778, coal mining, quarrying and metalworking were already established concerns, drawing labour from the improved lowlands and from further afield. Ships were leaving local ports for destinations on the continent, the Caribbean and the east coast of America.

The way of seeing that bracketed off the Lakes from these developments has affected our perception of the region ever since, much of the line reiterated with the foundation of the National Park in 1951. This can make it hard to appreciate how people frequently moved across the line, following traditions of living that were often extensive. There is no small irony in the fact that it is this idealised image of a small-scale and close-grained form of dwelling that still draws many visitors to the Langdales. Paths from distant places converging on the valley and the fells, a scale and complexity of connections completely at odds with the image itself.

The nature of the connections may have changed over time, but the interests and experience of those who have lived around the area have always stretched beyond the local horizon. And because of this, there has always been a variety to the tenure, the sense of attachment that people have recognised. In only a thousand years the Langdales have been marginal to some and valued to others; a focus for close relations and a place amongst many. Even a gift, offered in return for service or as strategy. Sometimes all of these at once.

The Langdales

A STRAGGLED HEAP OF UNHEWN STONES

Some of the earliest hints we have take the form of place names. The oldest of all may be Mickleden, 'large valley', which could date to between the seventh and ninth centuries, when Cumbria was part of the Anglian kingdom of Northumbria.[6] There are no recognised traces of settlement in the valley from that time. Though some of the high ground saw grazing or people moving through, the area was most likely regarded as of little value compared to the more extensively settled lowlands. Somewhere on the way, scrub on the slopes and woodland still common in the dale. How long things had been that way is debateable. Occasional artefacts and pollen suggest that the higher ground was also grazed in earlier centuries and many upland areas in Cumbria have evidence for settlement during the period of the Roman occupation. The Roman forts at Hardknott and Ambleside are also less than a day's walk away, the road between them running through Little Langdale.[7] In spite of this, there is as yet no strong signature of earlier settlement in the valley. Only time and further work will tell.

A stronger presence is not registered until the tenth century and the period of Norse or Anglo-Scandinavian settlement. Names like those that end with '-thwaite', a clearing, hint at an opening up of the cover. Some names are a combination of Old Norse and Old English. Langdale itself, 'long valley', has roots in both, first mentioned as 'Langdene' in 1179. Nearby, areas like Oxendale, 'the valley of the ox', are Old Norse, and a similar origin may lie behind the farm of Baysbrown, an inversion of the old Norse of *Bass* (cowshed) and *Bruni*, someone's name. There are other names as well, some Old Norse, others later, reflecting the persistence of the language in the local dialect.

The Old Norse names mark more than just a presence. References to cattle are common, and it is likely that communities of the time put stock onto the fells in some numbers. This probably involved sheep as well as cattle, the Herdwicks popularly held to have arrived with Norse settlers. The breed may in fact be older but whatever the balance, the tenth century saw an expansion into areas like Langdale, onto land seen as marginal by lowland populations who relied more heavily on arable. Part of existing aristocratic estates, it was well suited to pastoralism and was given to incomers as a form of patronage for which loyalty, rent and other services were expected in return. This is suggested by names in the area that have associations with Old Norse words for shielings, sites that were used as part of a seasonal pattern of stock transhumance.[8] Names with derivations of *skali, saetr* and *erg* occur at places like Rosset and Scale Gill, suggesting that the head of the valley and the higher fells were used in this way. Pavey Ark, above Stickle Tarn, may also be Old Norse, 'Pavey' a derivation of a person's name and 'Ark' a reworked form of *erg*. Some identifiable buildings on higher ground are probably tied to this time. The circular and rectangular footings of stone structures, and sometimes small

Along the Ringarth

Cairns and robbed walls above Wall End Farm

The Langdales

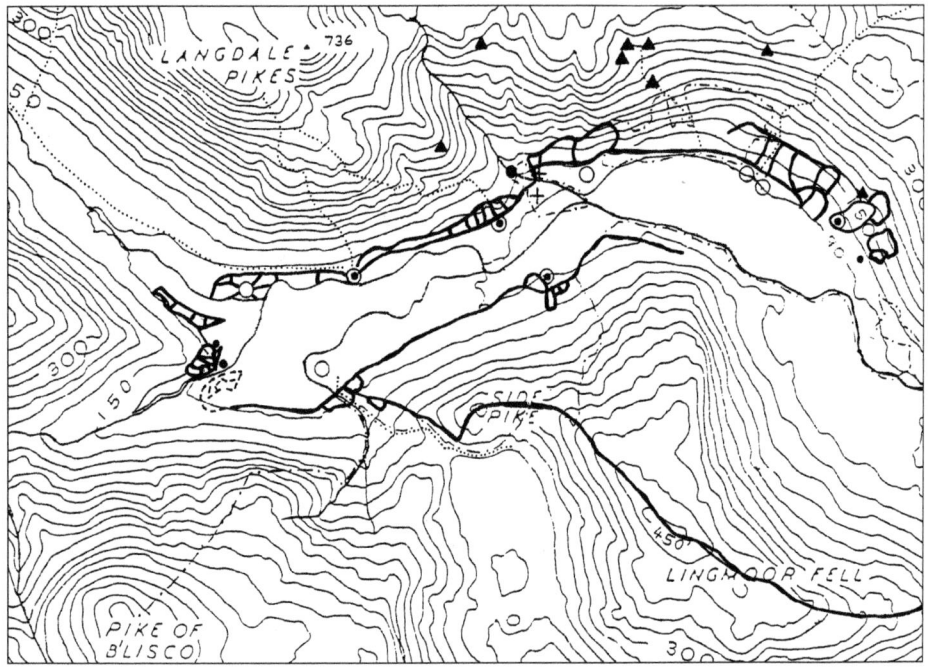

By the fifteenth century, new intakes had started to bite into the fellside, more farms on the break of the slope and peat huts higher up on the north side of the valley. Source: National Trust

Opposite *At the top of the intake*

enclosures, can be found in several areas, near Scale Ghyll, around Stickle Tarn and in Langdale Coombe. Notoriously difficult to date, even when excavated, some are later, reflecting the continued importance of upland pasture for many centuries. Some may even be older, dating to the later stages of prehistory. However, a few at least are likely remnants of this time, when sections of the community moved with their stock to take advantage of water and seasonal pasture on higher ground.

A similar pattern can be traced in Little Langdale, in place names such as Lingmoor – 'the heather covered hill', and in references to clearings and shielings. There are also several references to 'bields', isolated stretches of walling or rock formations that provided shelter for stock in rough weather. Names that describe the land, its uses and connections to people. The valley also contains another feature that dates to this time, though here, the references were probably broader. At its western end, by Fell Foot Farm on the banks of the Brathay, stands a substantial terraced mound. Built in the shadow of Castle Howe, the name of the crag perhaps a reference, this is most likely a Norse Moot Mount or 'Thingmount'. Documentary sources suggest that 'Thingmounts' were important meeting places, where people gathered to make decisions or pass judgement. On those occasions, the terraces may have

served to differentiate people, the higher spaces the preserve of those of a more elevated status, their subordinates beneath them on the lower tiers. Lying close to water and on a good route of access, the mound below Castle Howe was well placed to bring a broader community together.⁹

We know little in detail beyond these fragments; there are few traces of dwellings or related structures. Some of the cairns and banks that lie beyond the western limit of the modern walls in Mickleden could be contemporary, but could equally be far older. The same goes for the low banks and enclosures between Raw Pike and Castle How, high up on the north side of the valley. The footings of other buildings may also lie beneath more recent farms. What is certain is that the people who lived in and around the valley were not isolated. They may have been given land classed as marginal and low status and perhaps were regarded in the same way, but for them, the valley and fells were a focus, a living and, with time, a way of life. A breathing in and out of people from winter to summer. Not only that, they were bound to other parts of the region by ties of kinship and allegiance and by trade to complement their produce. Ties of loyalty at a distance, of reciprocity with those from a neighbouring valley who shared the higher fells. Obligations to pay rent and give service when required, revenue from the valley lining the coffers of aristocratic landlords in the lowlands. And beyond this, a sense of origins that could be traced across the water to Ireland and to Scandinavia. Ethnicity remembered in the names given to the land, a sense of difference that fed tensions in the region for a time before becoming part of its fabric.

Records are equally sparse for the following two centuries; a period that saw parts of Cumbria absorbed into the Kingdom of Strathclyde and the Norman Conquest. However, it is likely that whatever else they may have done, the aristocracies of the time grafted themselves onto an existing order, the boundaries of many estates and administrative districts already in place before their arrival. In the wake of the Conquest, the Langdale area was identified as 'Forest' within the Barony of Kendale. It is also likely that as in other upland valleys, Langdale saw an expansion of settlement, with new land assarted, walled and taken into cultivation, by individual farmsteads. By the early thirteenth century, this was a landscape worked by tenant farmers with customary rights of access, who paid rent of one sort or another to an aristocratic landlord.

Like many uplands, the pattern of settlement in Langdale was largely dispersed, individual tenants having a good deal of autonomy in terms of how they actually worked and developed land. Unlike many of the more nucleated villages and open fields in low-lying areas, the pattern of life had as much, if not more, to do with relations between tenants in the valley community as it did with an absent lord. Around 1216, the Baron of Kendal, one William de Lancaster, is recorded granting the land around 'Basebrun' to Conishead Priory, part of the valley rendered as a gift. Elements of the manorial boundary established around this time can still be traced in the line of Great Langdale

Beck and the River Brathay, and as walling (some of it rebuilt much later) between Lingmoor and Wall End. Farms established by then include Middlefell Place, Rossett, Harry Place, Robinson Place and Baysbrown. Some had seen use in the Norse period; others were established by later encroaching on the forest, enclosing irregular intakes within field walls such as those near Stool End, Sidehouse and Robinson Place.[10]

From then onwards, walls take on a particular importance in accounts, none more so than the Ring Garth.[11] Still traceable today, elements of the Ring Garth or Ring Fence were probably established around the tenth or eleventh century, a more or less continuous boundary running along the break of slope between valley floor and steeper fellsides. Boulders weighing several tons dragged into position, smaller slates and cobbles stacked above shoulder height. A communal undertaking. Many farms were also placed at this level, to avoid the threat of flooding and to take advantage of resources up and downslope. Tracks were consolidated along a similar line, carrying people from one household to another, then onwards, beyond the valley. Stretches of the modern road perpetuate the same division between low ground and fellside, the Ring Garth surviving upslope as walling and as foundations where stone has been robbed for later walls.

This boundary served several purposes. It drew a line between the low ground where crops were grown, and the slopes where animals grazed, keeping

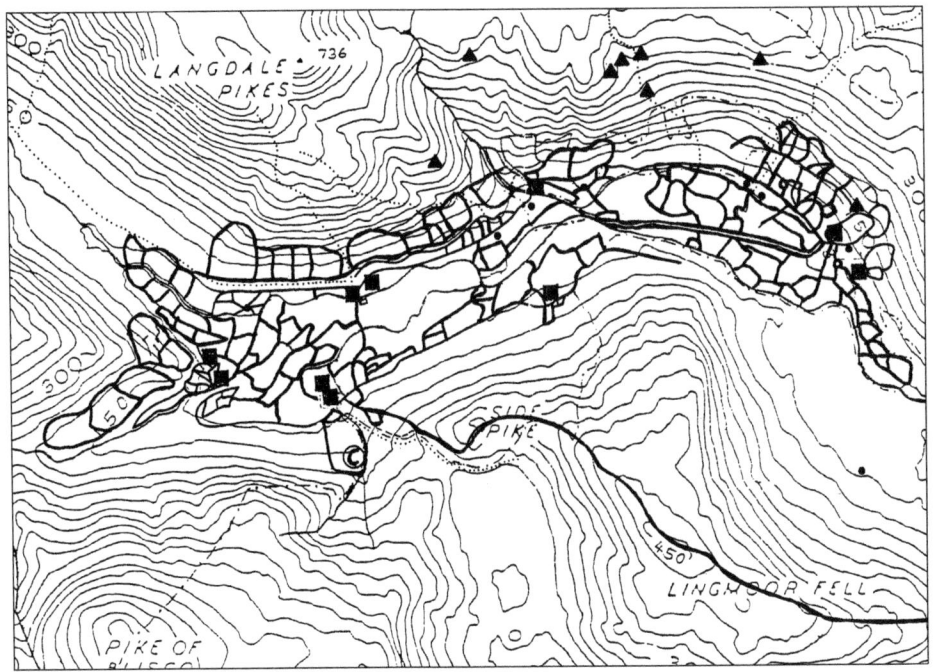

From the later sixteenth to mid-eighteenth century, statesmen farmers, cottagers and other tenants made further claims on common ground. Tenements grew in number and land was enclosed on the flat as well as on the fell, rights of access defined by walled outrakes. Source: National Trust

Opposite *The Nick Stick Seat*

the two apart in certain seasons. Within its line, land was cultivated by individual farms and as common field, areas worked collectively or in shares, labour and produce divided between several families. Most families also had smaller individual fields or crofts immediately around their farms. Beyond, the stock could fatten on the fellsides, growing accustomed to particular slopes in a process known locally as heafing. Though paths overlapped, each farm had its own heaf, a tract of open country on which sheep generally remained. All that heafing required was a measure of continuity in stock from one generation to the next.

> . . . *I thought the slaughter would spread to the fells and if we'd lost the Herdwicks that would have been it for me. The compensation would have been something. But none of us have the time or money we'd've needed to get new stock set . . . Can you imagine all the fencing on the fells, even on the tops. They might have helped us out but I don't know they'd've allowed it . . .*

The Ring Garth also had a more directly political role. It drew a line between the inbye land, where tenants grew their crops, and the common or waste on the fellsides, held as the Lord's demesne. Far from waste, these uplands were highly valued by the manorial lords or monastic houses who held them. Beyond timber and minerals, they provided revenue from rent, or through more direct use. In several valleys, they were worked as 'vaccaries', large-scale ranches where cattle were run for the estate by the medieval equivalent of cowboys. In Langdale, tenants paid an 'agistment' for the right to pasture, peat and bracken across the fellside, customary payments made to the Lord's Bailiff at the 'Nick Stick Seat' – incorporated into a wall below Robinson Place. The name refers to a tally stick, used for counting and as a token of contract when labour was hired; half each retained by employer and hand. The administration of these arrangements is a key theme in medieval and later documents relating to the area. Records identify disputes arising from non-payment of rents or the unwarranted enclosure of parts of the fellside by farmers who, in spite of heafing, sought to keep stock, particularly cattle, closer to home.

Langdale did not escape the decline in population and economic fortune that hit home in the early decades of the fourteenth century; a consequence of poor harvests, plague and the loss of stock to diseases like rinderpest and murrain. There was also the threat of raiding, though this impacted more directly elsewhere in the region. Records talk of a reduction of tenanted land, of insufficient corn to keep the mills going throughout the year, and of men from the valley called into service to act as border guards against raids from Scotland. Empty holdings, land turning back to scrub, anxiety over a loved one's safe return. It was not until the later fifteenth century that growth returned, putting pressure on land and encouraging expansion. Additional farms were established from this time onwards, and new ground was brought into cultivation. Walls were built running upslope from the Ring Garth to intake land that was then cleared, stone incorporated into the walls or piled into cairns. Fields dating to this time can be seen around Stool End and Wall End, the grass of cleared ground generally greener than the unimproved land beyond.

Several mills were also in operation, some on old foundations. A corn mill in Langdale appears in documents as early as the thirteenth century, and over the years the number increased, additional mills for corn and for fulling – the processing of woollen cloth. Not all can be located. The farm at Millbeck, near the lower end of Stickle Ghyll, stands close to the site of a mill for which rents were being paid in the sixteenth century, while another was established at Elterwater Hall. The fulling sites, which gave a local alternative to established mills in Grasmere, demonstrate the importance of wool and cloth for the valley community. Wool was worked at home, often spun by women and then woven by men. It was then taken off for sale in Hawkshead or more distant towns like Kendal, where it was dyed and exported.

Opposite *On the Rossett path. Turning back upon itself to ease the pace of the descent, the track still shifts as stretches are redirected to slow the pace of erosion*

Opposite *Outrake*

> *... In the winter it used to be different. No one for days and you're in so early ... too much time to think ... now there's folk all over the year ...*

Surveys prompted by changes of ownership at the dissolution in the mid-sixteenth century point to a substantial population in the valley – a community large enough to warrant two chapels and a reader, and a strong presence at the church in Grasmere. Many from the valley made the journey over the tops each Sunday, the north aisle of the church known through customary use as the 'Langdale side'. When they died, their bodies made the journey again, along the 'Wake walk' or corpse road from Walthwaite and Huntingstile for burial on consecrated ground. Others were carried to Hawkshead, Christian burial in the valley becoming routine only when the church and graveyard replaced the chapel at Chapel Stile in the nineteenth century. It wasn't always that way; some were buried in the valley much earlier. At Oak Howe Farm on the darker side of the dale, records suggest that along with several others, one Anthony Dixon was buried close by in 1579; immediate interment a response to an outbreak of plague.

Chapel congregations grew, and the sixteenth century saw the further division of tenanted land, as growing families established secondary tenements. Now identified as a single holding, the farm at Robinson Place takes in several;

The Langdales

Borderstone, Pye Howe, Ellers and Cowshot Howe among them. This brought problems of access to the common field and difficulties when stock needed moving between the low ground and the higher fellsides. Good walls did not always make good neighbours. Farms sometimes fell into dispute over the maintenance and respect of walls and rights of way and as a consequence, long established paths were augmented by outrakes. Often walled on the low ground, these defined rights of movement for both people and stock. Many survive and are still in use; others are incorporated into footpaths, the walking boot replacing the hoof. Boundaries also required negotiation, wallheads marking the point along a line where the responsibility for upkeep shifted from one farm to another. This was an ongoing and protracted process.[12] Over many years, it bound people to each other as well as to the land, lines of descent recognised in clusters of tenements, in ways of walling and on the backs and ears of sheep. A network of relations that shifted through marriage and inheritance, that came into focus in the pews of the local chapel and on the tombstones in Grasmere and Hawkshead.

It was out of these conditions that the 'statesmen' emerged. These were independent smallholders who, by virtue of accrued capital, marriage or gifts for service, held a secure tenure on parcels of land. To all intents and purposes freeholders, these more independent farmers continued the trend of intaking

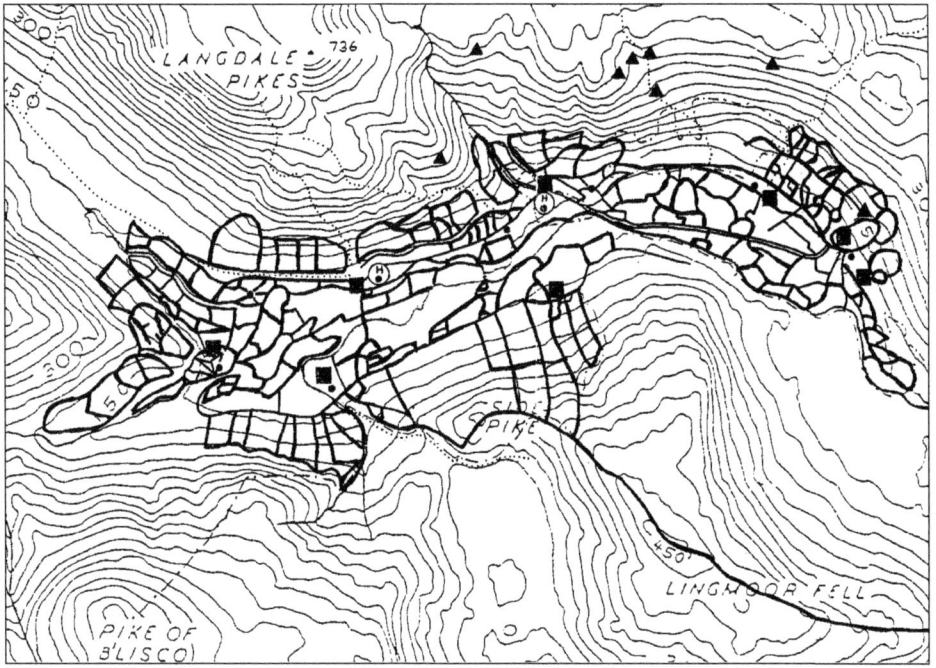

The Age of Improvement saw a reduction in the number of tenements and an increase in the scale of individual holdings. In keeping with the spirit of the times, new enclosures on the south side of the valley tended more towards the regular. Source: National Trust

land from the later sixteenth century onwards. Fortunes still shifted. Plague and a decline in the woollen industry hit home again in the seventeenth century, broader shifts of fashion causing a local tightening of belts and a push into work like mining and quarrying. But the statesmen maintained a pattern to landholding, access and communication that was to persist some way into the eighteenth century, providing a model of hardy independence that would later be romanticised by visitors and the writers of guides. Adding further fields to those already existing beyond the Ring Garth, they consolidated much of the organic pattern of enclosures that we can still see today, each field named. Bacabeck, Wood Hinning, Gala field, Wet Parrock, Big Bitts and Ash Busk; the list is a long one. Sit on Raw Pike or Oak How Needle and you can trace the walls of these enclosures in several directions. Things also changed downslope, parts of the common field enclosed from this time onwards to serve the interests of particular farms, which were themselves rebuilt and extended. Many of the buildings in use today have seventeenth- or early eighteenth-century roots.

By the time that Wordsworth himself was singing their praises, the number of statesmen had begun to dwindle.[13] Many individual tenements were once again amalgamated into larger holdings as a consequence of recession and the drive to accumulate land by a growing gentry. Some of the farmsteads abandoned at this time became 'hogg houses' or cow byres, others were dismantled for use in new walls. When the light is right, you can sometimes see the platforms on which they stood, nowhere more clearly than in the fields opposite the cruck barn at Wall End Farm. By the mid-eighteenth century, the farming of the valley was divided between a smaller number of holdings, and it was against this background that those with due title, in keeping with the fashion of the day, experimented with improvement. New crops were introduced, new drains were cut, attempts made to control the volatile seasonal flow of water off the fells. There were new enclosures too, rationalisations of land in larger and more regular fields such as those that bisect Side Pike, or subdivide the slopes above Wall End. Often starting life as plans on a surveyor's drawing board, these more geometric fields appealed to improvers. More easily measured, they allowed the close calculation of areas and yields and in turn, the fixing of value. In places, they helped draw a line across customary forms of access and use that had gone largely unchallenged for generations. Authority identified directly in the land.[14]

The impact of these developments in Great Langdale was significant, but by no means as dramatic as it might have been, still less in Little Langdale. The number and variety of tenements made it difficult to impose the more draconian changes seen in lowland areas, where vast swathes of land were held and 'improved' by a single owner. The terrain didn't help either and this encouraged the continued survival of many older features. The land also set a pattern in another way. By the mid-eighteenth century, tourists were already making their way up Stake Pass and into the valley to view and sketch the 'classic ground'. A new kind of stock to manage.[15]

> . . . yeah . . . it was in the papers a few years ago, my daughter sent the clipping back from college . . . an exhibition of photographs, in London wasn't it? . . . Just snaps a woman had taken of a holiday in the lakes with her mates. Thing is though, they were all black weren't they . . . I live in town so I'd not thought about it like that . . . makes no odds to me . . . but it was strange, out on the fells like that . . . like there was a fence that some couldn't cross . . . [11]

WHAT TIME IS THIS PLACE?

One of the attractions of a place like Langdale is the richness of the evidence around the fields and on the fells. With a little time, the eye can soon pick out the order in which certain enclosures were added to others, spot a different build or an older cairnfield scattered out beyond the intakes. The terrain and the history of holdings have made it hard for new brooms to sweep the land entirely clean. What will always be more difficult is catching the lives that lie behind those features. That may be why we fall back so readily upon romance, seeing those lives as no more complex than the 'straggled heap of unhewn stones' that caught Wordsworth's eye. But people were seldom isolated; they were a part of many communities. Those who shared the higher seasonal fells, who respected customary rights and 'met half way' to exchange lost sheep with commoners from Borrowdale or Eskdale. Those who span or quarried together, who worked side by side in the 'town field', or protested as one against an increase in rent. People bound by a moral economy. And all of this within broader worlds that often consigned the valley to the margins. Tribal, monastic and secular lords; service, sermons and bailiffs. Demands for wool, for cloth and minerals, even for labour in shifting dual economies; transactions which carried goods and people in and out of the valley. To market or to work elsewhere, seasons on the border, at a rockface, or up with the stock. Life has often involved an expectation of tasks and journeys, of different places and varied companies.

What the area meant more than four thousand years before the fells acquired Norse names is still harder to imagine. People recognised strong ties, but attention was focused on the high ground and the crags, not on the break of slope where more recent settlement tends to run. It was also based upon a different sense of tenure, one that did not depend upon sustained occupation. For communities of the Neolithic, Langdale was not just a particular place; it was also a particular time.

That was how it was across much of Cumbria. During the fourth millennium and for some time after, the landscapes of the region bore little relation to what we see today. Life strung out between clearings or along the edges of the canopy. There was ground with a long history of occupation and other places only seen or used from time to time. Families scattered across the lower Furness Peninsula or up the coast at Drigg often travelled further afield. To marshy land where reeds and fowl could be had; to higher and more open country where the grazing and the game were good. And when the time was right and the sea allowed, there were even longer journeys. The annual cycle saw people moving along broad corridors of land that linked the coastal plains or the valley sides of the east with the higher country of the fells. Moving stock and tending to plots, collecting honey, bark or hazelnuts; tasks stretched across summer and winter ground and along rivers and watersheds. The land was a patchwork on which work never ceased.

Life was also dispersed; common companies no more than an extended family or even smaller groups. Time spent where familiar talk was broken only by the waves, or by the sounds of work and spirits in the woods. Within these conditions, places acquired genealogies; read in the condition of the country and fostered in oral tradition, woven into origin myths and broader senses of an ancestral past. Simply following customary paths was a form of respect paid to country, a way of renewing a connection with places and with their past. Where tensions arose, they often revolved around the breaking of those paths.

And where work possessed the qualities of custom, it fostered an awareness of this world; its character, roots and why it mattered. A child learning how to split planks or cut poles also learnt about the history behind the timber, the genealogies traceable in a managed stand. Another learning to burn scrub, to read the sea or the high ground, heard stories of origins and of more extensive relations. Communities from another valley, from across the water or further up the coast. A broader world that turned in talk around the fires of evening hearths. A world carried in the objects exchanged into different valleys and in the blood of animals.

This wider geography came into sharp relief when people worked alongside others, or gathered at a sacred site. When paths crossed as a matter of course, and when tradition dictated that people came together. It was often because of these broader relations that things changed. Marriages between lines, tensions over access, inheritance and the settlement of disputes; each brought subtle shifts in the contours of social life. Obligations incurred and renown accrued through feasting or exchange might lead some to wield a local authority, just as elders might claim priority over the young. A certain standing may have also come to those who made the journey there and back across the sea. There were no doubt even times when claim and counter-claim led to feuding, raiding and other forms of conflict. Arguments over land, stock or access to a trail; a matter of blood that had run for many years; disrespect shown to the spirits of a place. That was how it was; the playing out of relations between lines that twisted across generations.

This mixing of the local and the more extensive left its mark on the Langdales. In the fourth millennium, it was somewhere that required a journey from more familiar and more sedimented country. Not then lived in all year round, it received small groups of people who travelled for the grazing as well as for the stone. But even here, the broader world was important. There is no reason to assume that stonework required isolation, certainly not the isolation valued so jealously by the Romantics and many since then. The hornstone was well placed to be approached from several directions and this was significant for the ways the crags were regarded. The source drew you up at certain times. But it drew others up as well; paths overlapped here. Stone on the flanks of Scafell could be reached from the Esk or by following one of the ghylls from Wasdale up towards Lord's Rake. It was thus accessible from the western lowlands and the coast. Langdale too could be reached without hardship from the west. Paths from the crags also run to the south, to the coast or across towards the Eden Valley and the Pennines. There is also a path from the north, once a major packhorse route; through Borrowdale and along Langstrath, then rising to retrace the steps of the water running down Stake Beck. Maintained by revetments and pitching, this was an important route until the development of the turnpikes in the mid-eighteenth century. By then, it was also a favoured tourist path, the modern Cumbria Way taking the same line to this day.

On high ground valued now by many because of the chance it seems to offer of escape from others, it is difficult to conceive of such a different view. The task is not made any easier by names. One of the more subtle implications that flows when we call these sources 'Axe Factories' is that the labour and the stone were full-time and exclusively owned. This is probably wrong. What evidence there is suggests a periodic and probably seasonal pattern of small groups making journeys to work for a time. And though people would have identified closely with particular parts of the outcrop, rights of access extended far beyond the horizons of a single extended family. In fact, this was one part of the region where visits necessarily required regular contact and communication, a familiarity with the wider web of relationships within which families were set.[16] You had to know where it was appropriate and customary to take stone. You had to know the stories and the histories of the crags and to show these respect in the manner of your approach. If you didn't know, you had to be instructed. How to seek a blessing from important spirits; how to offer gifts to the stone. The time also had to be right and not just because of the grazing. Others had to agree and perhaps mark their consent by participation. Because of this, tensions that arose elsewhere could make themselves felt in arguments over where and when it was appropriate to work. Beyond the drama of the crags, the climb and the stone itself, the area was prominent because it required attention to a wider community.

> . . . we're all immigrants really aren't we . . . I'm Cumbrian I guess, but my dad's family moved from Glasgow in the twenties to work in the yards. Does that make me Scots or English? I don't know . . . weren't there loads of Vikings here? . . .

The Langdales were not the only area where paths overlapped. There were many places where concepts of the past and of a broader world were prominent in local imaginations; among them what we call tombs. Sites like Skelmore Heads in Low Furness, Raiset Pike in the Eden Valley or Sampsons Bratful on the western flank of Stockdale Moor.[17] There are others as well, long since destroyed on improved ground, or waiting to be identified amongst the rock outcrops, later cairns and earthworks that litter shelves between the plains and the high country. Places like Trainford Brow, Heathwaite, Irton or Mossthorn. The small number of tombs we do know of are poorly understood. Few have been excavated and those that have are not blessed with the best of records. Long cairns or accumulations of smaller mounds, they have nonetheless revealed an association with the dead; remains sometimes disarticulated and even burnt in interior features. At Raiset Pike, Canon Greenwell found a number of disarticulated bodies in a thin trench beneath a mound around 60 metres in length. At the south-east end, these bones had been burnt *in situ*, vertical flues ventilating the fires.[18] Similar examples of this practice were identified at Lamb's Crag in the south west, as well as further afield in both Yorkshire and Ireland. Local variations on broader traditions. There were also other ways of dealing with the dead. In some parts of the region, the Neolithic saw the exposure of bodies on outcrops and low stone platforms. Some of these were reworked as burial mounds towards the end of the period, but the limited amount of work done so far means that we do not know just how far back their foundations go.

Just how these different monuments were regarded is difficult to say. More detailed work in other regions warns against treating each tomb as a singular structure. Many are actually accumulations of episodes; visited, embellished and remodelled over long sequences. The surface appearance of Sampson's Bratful or the cairns at Crosby Garrett suggests that this was also the case here, that some tombs were used, respected and re-used over several generations at least. That work also suggests a variety to events and settings and this was probably so in Cumbria. Tombs built on land grazed in common, near important resources or by sites with long histories of occupation.[19] It is also likely that some were established in named places, ridges, outcrops and springs associated with stories of the origins of the land and the actions of ancestral beings. To the west of the fells, the setting of several cairns suggests that they were on the edges of land where grazing complemented hunting and gathering. They are also on the threshold between the lower and higher ground, well placed for an encounter when people moved onto higher ranges at certain times. Some were probably passed or even visited by those on longer journeys to the hornstone.

Tombs were probably not a resting place for all. Many paths carried people into the afterlife; exposure, the dispersal of bones or ashes in woodland, the consigning of the dead to rivers or to the sea. Rites were often complex and protracted, tombs sometimes no more than a station in the process. Local dealings with the dead may have often revolved around other rites and different places, ones that we might recognise as natural; on the shore, or on exposed and prominent crags. It may be more than a coincidence that sites like Crosby Garrett in the Eden Valley incorporate striking rocky outcrops in their fabric; perhaps these were already significant before the first cairn was raised. The same may apply to many of the caves and fissures that are common on the limestone in the region; places like Dog Hole Cave near Carnforth, Kirkhead Cave near Allithwaite or the Bonfire Cave at Scales in Furness. Passage linked to stories of distant worlds, or to the spirits that dwelt within the land.[20]

The fragments of the dead identified by Greenwell also have their parallels. There are tombs where bones arrived already stripped of their flesh; exposed or defleshed elsewhere. In other cases, decay and disarticulation took place within the tomb itself, the breaking up and sorting of bones happening only after that process had run its course. The make up of body parts in several tombs also suggests that sometimes bones went out as well as in, carried away to circulate amongst the living or for burial elsewhere. It is in this emphasis on collective deposits that archaeologists often trace a community of dead kin who looked over and after the living. This is probably simplistic. Rites that appear to evoke a sense of community in death could conceal important differences of identity and authority. However, inclusion, even for a time, may have been a privilege of kinship and descent, bones or bodies brought to a tomb by a handful of extended families who knew the names of those who lay within. Whether this was the case in Cumbria we do not know for sure. Certainly, the firing of collective deposits and their burial beneath a covering mound brought access to a close. But even when this happened, mounds often continued as a focus for ritual activity. By descendants who knew the names of the dead; by others, who laid claim to an ancestral house as a way of laying claim to other things.

For the communities who built and used them, tombs connected present and past, a line traced in the rhetoric of rituals at each site. They bound people together through a shared communion, gathering in the shadow of a tomb at certain times of year or when a death prompted a return. As some mingled around tasks nearby, others attended to proceedings. The handling of dry bone; acts of oratory and preparations for a meal in the presence of the dead. Labour in company, chains of hands piling one stone upon another; axes swung to cut timbers and planks. Where the fertility of land and people was in the gift of spirits, these periodic gatherings were important. To ensure good crops and

Enclosure walls running up by Side Pike

healthy herds; to renew links with land and with others through reference to the past. More besides. The crossing of many thresholds required sanction from the dead. What also mattered was that threads came together. The range may not have been as great as that recognised from time to time around the Langdales. But horizons still lifted beyond those of the extended family. Tombs were therefore places where exchange could be anticipated and even required. A new marriage between families; the sorting out of rights and responsibilities on the death of an elder. Each of these could be addressed through the handing on or handing down of important tokens. And when people came together there was a chance for other transactions, for the renewal of bonds that would lead to trade in the months ahead. Here too was a chance to decide if the time was right to return to the outcrop, to seek sanction for the venture from those who had made the journey years before.

andromeda – andy pandy – angel heart – ann's agony – annie's song – another bleeding cor ash tree slabs – ash tree slabs direct – ashen traverse – ask ted – assault and matrimony – as route – b.b – corner – baby blue sky – babylon – bachelor crack – baldy's wall – banks beckham's blunder – before the storm – belly ache – ben – bentley – big brother – big jim black wars – blade runner – blake rigg – blandish – blea crag – blea rigg climb – bleaber easons – borstal buttress – bowfell – bowfell buttress – bowfell buttress eliminate – bowfell damnation – brain damage – bravado – brazen hussey – breaking point – brian stalin – bridg rousers – bryson's flange – bryson's picnic – bumble arete – by-pass route – c route – camb – cascade – cascade direct – casket – cave buttress – centipede – centipede direct – central – chopper – clag men – clare – cliff at christmas – close shave – clothes show – cold night he sky – crack – crackpot – cravat – crazy horse – crescent climb – crescent direct – cresce – crinkle gill – crooked crack – crow's nest direct – cruel sister – crustacean traverse – cry damascus – dancin' barefoot – dangerous dave's mud trip – dave's arete – dawes rides a s groove – death camp – death star – deceiver – deception – deer bield crag – demonic elim ot direct – doberman – dodgy d – don't look back – doolittle – dot's delight – dream – dre crag – easedale – easedale groove – easedale ramble – east buttres girdle – east raven crag elterwater quarries – elton john – elvis – enormous room – enterprize – equus – erne – eth oute – fallen angel – far east raven crag – far from the stickle barn – fastburn – fat boys cra ouch – flarepath – flarepath direct – flat crag corner – flat crags – flat crags climb – flat iro squirrel – forget me not – forrudd – frankie goes to kendal – fruit bat – fun run – furtive sor – gentle touch – gibli – gibson knott – gilette direct – gimmer chimney – gimmer crag – gi glamourpus ghuru – glass clogs – glass slipper – gordian knot – gotama – graduate – grand – grey rib – grip trip – gripsville – grondle grooves – groove arete – grooves superdirect – g hang the gallows high – hanging corner – hanging knotts – hardup wall – harrison stickle – – heads call – heart of the matter – heartbreaker – heartsong – heather groove – heather sla hidden secrets – hidden treasure – highlander – hitcher – hobbit – hobson's choice – hog hollywood babylon – hope beyond hoping – horror – hot aches – hotpot – hubball groove mpact day – inertia – inferno – inspiration – interlude – intern – into the light – introduc ingo – joas – joker's slab – jolly corner – jolly roger – judith – junction arete – jungle wa on keeping on – kelly's crack – kettle crag – kipling groove – kneewrecker chimney – kudo ast tango – laugh not – ledge and groove – ledged wall – left chimney – left ridge – left wa ittle corner – little gully – little jack – long scar – longhair – looking howe crag – lordy mi main wall rib – main wall scoop – maintenance chimney – major slab – mamba – man of nary ann – mega pitch – men at work – mendes – mendes traverse – merlin slab – mice – no fixed abode – mindbender – minder – mindprobe – minor slab – mithrandir – monkey crack – muscle wall – musgrave's traverse – mussolini – mystery crack – mythical m.m – na arete – needle – nelli kim – neurotics – new partnership – nineveh – no big cigar – no flan – north west arete – northern territories – not again – nutcracker cleft – oak how crag – oa slab – oh heck direct – old holborn – old man's crack – oliverson's variation and lyons' darkness – outside tokyo/dight – oyster rib – paladin – paleface – palestinians – pallid sla swine – peascod's route – pendulum – peppered boursin – perhaps not – perplexity – ph platt gang groove – pluto – poacher – poacher right hand – pocket crack – pocket rocket – – potty – power of imagination – pragmatic – pratinacar – prelude – press gang/olga kor professor of pulchritude – prophet – proportional representation – protus – prow – public aindancer – rainmaker – rake end chimney – rake end wall – rambler's hangover – ramp walthwaite – raven girdle – ray parker is innocent – razor crack – razor's edge – real worl remains of the day – remembrance – return of the giant hogweed – revelation – rhythm oute – right wall eliminate – right hand chimney – right hand wall – risus – riverboat ga oute 1, raven walthwaite – route 1, scout crags – route 1, tarn crag – route 1, gibson knott knott – route one – rowan tree groove – roy rogers – rubicon groove – rudolf nureyef – r samaritan corner – samarkand – savernake – scabbard – scared rabbit – scoop – scout cr from the storm – shivering timber – shizen groove – short cut – short man's route – showe – singing cowboy – sinister footwear – sinister slabs – sinistral – sixpence – skinhead – sk – sleep on my pillow – sleeping soldiers – slim buttress arete – slim crack – slip knot – south-east gully – south-east lower traverse – speckled band – spectrum – spider crack – stalag – stars and bars – startrek – stephen – steve's groove – stewpot – stickle barn crag street legal – strop – stubble – subsidiary ridge – sunshine crack – supernova – swastika damocles – tapestry – tarn crag – tattered banners – tenderfoot – terrace crack – terrace buttress – tonsor – tonsure – too bleeding hard – too excess – tower climb – tracheotomy ed – ultimate extension – uncle george – upper spout crag – v chimney – v chimney are sunshine – walkington's tour – wall end – waller's crack – walthwaite crack – walthwaite – west buttress – west raven crag – west wall – what not – whit's end – whit's end direct – white ghyll wall – white rabbit – why not – wide boy – wilkinson's sword – woolly jumpe sy – antarctica – aragorn – arcturus – arete crack – armadillo – armalite – ash tree corner – asterix the gaul – astra – astral by-way – ataxia – atmospheric phenomena – axe the tax – barry's traverse – basher's bulge – baskerville – beacon crack – beacon rib – beatles buttress – bilko – bill – billy bunter – bimbo boffin – bitter days – black crag – black slab ress – blind – blondie – blood on the tracks – blue remembered day – bob dylan – book of s girdle – bowfell links – bracken route – bracken clock – bracket and slab climb – bradley's riation – bright beck corner – bright beck crag – british bulldogs – brocken spectre – brown climb – cambridge crag – campaign crack – cape fear – capella – carpetbagger – cartwheel centrefold – chameleon – chequer buttress – cheroot – chimney buttress – chimney variant na – comatose – confidence trick – confusion wall – cook's tour – cooper crack – crack in s – crescent superdirect – crescent wall – crimes of quality – crinkle corner – crinkle crags ub's arete – cub's crack – cub's groove – cub's wall – cut-throat – d route – d.g – corner – ead – dead loss angeles – deadlock – deadly dave's demonic rib – deadly dave's demonic demonic rib and wall – detour – deuterus – digitalis – dilemna – dinsdale – dipthong – do chants – dry rain – dunmail cracks – dunn cruisin' – dusk crack – dynamo – e route – eagle ern hammer – eclipse – eden groove – edge of darkness – ee-by-gum – efrafa – eliminot – war – eulogy – evening wall – evensong – ex captain webb and the lioness – exposure – f her of night – feet of clay – festerday – fine art of surfacing – fine time – finger swing – first – flattery – flight of the bumble bee – flower pot man – flying blind – flying glasses – flying mekeeper – gandalf's groove direct – gandhi – gareth – geneva convention – genital touch orilla – gimmer high girdle – gimmer string – girdle traverse – gizzard – gladstone knott – granny knot – granny knot direct – great gully – green gambit – green light – grey corner traverse – grouter – gunson knott – gwynne's chimney – gymslip – half moon – hand line icklefront – harristickorner and spilikin ridge – hash 'n' trash – haste not – haste not direct lo helen – helm crag – herdwick buttress – hermann goering – hiatus – hidden pleasures – rect – hold on – hollin groove – holly tree crack – holly tree direct – holly tree traverse – is – hunted – hyphen – i crashed a vulcan bomber – idle breed – iguana – imagination – ntruder's corner – it's now or never – ivory wall – jagged edge – jerusalem – jim's route – all gully – juniper buttress – kalashnikov – karma – karma kings – katie's dilemna – keep ally – langdale cowboys – langdale cowboys continuation – langdale ferrets – last corner – ngrad – lichen groove lightning crag – limbo – limpet grooves – lingmoor – little acorns – madonna – maggie's farm – main wall climb – main wall crack – main wall left hand marginality – margot fonteyn – marilyn 60 today – marilyn monroe please – marrawhack – ll buttress – midnight movie – militant tendency – millbeck crag – miller stands – mind of monkey the needle – moon shadow – moonglow – moss wall – mother courage – muscle urally demonic – navigator error – nazareth – neckband crag – neckband – nectar – needle poor – no rest for the wicked – nocturne – nod off – noddy – north buttress – north gully eedle – oak tree wall – obelix and co – oberon – obscured by clouds – odin – offcomers' lympus – ophidia – orange pekoe – orchid – original route – ornithology – out from the 's wall – panatella – party animal – patella pinch – pathfinder – pavey ark – pearls before 's climb – pianissimo – pianola – pike of blisco – pike of stickle – pillar – pink panties – ay – poker face – pollster – porkers parade – porphyry slab – porridge – potluck – pottering tty in pink – prey – private affair – private dancer – private eye – private investigations nce – pump and strain – pump up the pillar – r'n's special – ragman's trumpet – rainbow – ramrod – ramsbottom variation – raven crag buttress – raven crag langdale – raven crag nt – rectangular rib – rectangular slab – red groove – red slab – redundancy of courage – ib and wall – rib pitch – rib, friend zero and groove – rib – riboletto – right of peascod's ck around the clock – rope not – rope up – roundabout – roundabout direct – roundup – .5 – route 2, raven walthwaite – route 2, scout crags – route 2, tarn crag – route 2, gibsor russet groove – s.s.scoop – sahara – sally free and easy – salmon leap – sam's saunter t's belt – scrambler's corner – semerikod – sexpot – sharni slab – sharp as glass – shelte ation – shroud – siamese chimneys – side pike – sign of four – silent witness – simon say slab – slabs, route 1 – slabs, route 2 – slape stones – slapestone edge – slapheads groove ariations – slipshod – slowburn – solaris – solstice – something stupid – sooty – sorbo key – spider wall – spiny norman – spoof wall – sport for all – spout crag – springbank – rooves – stickle slab – stiletto – sting – stoat's crack – stony buttress – stop showing off – sweeney todd – sweep – swine knott – swing to the left – swing to the right – sword o ang crag – three – time after time – tinkerer – tinning's move – titania – titus groan – toe ina – trigger – trilogy – tritus – troll's corner – twilight stroll – twin cracks right – two sta on girdle traverse – veil – vertical invader – virgo – wailing wall – walk tall – walking or lthwaite gully left hand – warlock – warrior – waste not, want not – watch – watson wal – white ghyll chimney – white ghyll crag – white ghyll eliminate – white ghyll traverse e crack – yellow fever – yellow peril – young apprentice – zebedee – zero route.

On Gimmer. Photo: Nick Wharton

CHAPTER 6

STONEWORK

> *. . . if only those geologists would let me alone, I could do very well, but those dreadful hammers! I hear the clink of them at the end of every cadence of the Bible verses . . .*

John Ruskin was as troubled as he was fascinated by geology. Like many of his time and kind, he was a keen collector; of fossils and antiquities, but above all, of rocks and minerals. You can see them scattered around his home at Brantwood on the shores of Coniston. For Ruskin, the methods of the stripling science chimed with his aesthetic; a close examination of process and form, of the mountains that were 'the beginning and the end of all scenery'. After that, they parted company. The conclusions that geologists were drawing, their implication of deep time, threw up a challenge to his faith, a contradiction he struggled with for many years. More than this, their models and classifications seemed to him to scratch no more than the surface. Thin descriptions at best, there seemed no place for a sense of wonder, no poetic exploration to match Turner's vision.

It wasn't just geology that troubled Ruskin; he wasn't too keen on mountaineers either. As he struggled to catch the relation of humanity to what he saw as the most blessed manifestation of nature, others were bagging summits. He had little time for those who treated mountains as 'soaped poles in a bear garden'. For him, understanding came not from mere sensation, but from the cultivation of vision. A moral vision that could recognise the inestimable scale

of mountain processes, and something greater still, in even the smallest of fragments.

    Had he lived to read the literature that has grown up around climbing, Ruskin might have modified his views. He might have reluctantly acknowledged that close understanding arises from a mixture of senses rather than just vision. So can a sense of community.[1] The sport which, in Robert Graves' words, 'made all other sports seem trivial' has generated a wealth of literature in which this point is made. Work in the tradition of the Romantics by people like W.H. Murray, for whom the physical experience of the climb was a trigger for revelation. Essays which link the freedom to climb to broader demands for emancipation. There is even poetry which takes its form from individual routes, or more modernist experiments; strings of words to catch body and crag becoming one.

                  Opposite *Pillar*. Photo: Armitt Library

Climbing as an activity in its own right was established in Cumbria as Ruskin was gazing from his study window; some of the earliest routes put up on Pillar above Ennerdale and Napes Needle on Great Gable. The fells were not, of course, *terra incognita*. For local shepherds and for others, many crags were both named and familiar, something readily acknowledged even then. One of the Langdale logbooks contains a reference to Jack's Rake on Pavey Ark. Attributed to Pendlebury in the late nineteenth century, the description of the route goes on to note that '. . . the first recorded ascent of this course was made by Jack, *circa* 1400 AD. Will any member possessing evidence of any previous ascent kindly communicate with the editor . . .'. What mattered from Ruskin's time onwards was what could be made of the journey itself.[2]

At first, the fells were secondary; training grounds where those who could afford to be alpinists got in shape before tackling ascents elsewhere. But by the 1880s, climbs began to be established for their own sake by people like Owen Glynne Jones and Haskett Smith, who put up some of the earliest routes in the Langdales. Encouraged by guides and by the photography of the Abraham brothers from Keswick, the sport grew rapidly in the area, the 'Fell and Rock Climbing Club of the English Lake District' formed in 1906. Thousands of routes have since been put up across the region, each one named, attributed, and described in meticulous detail in collective logbooks. In Langdale, quite a few of these routes bear the name 'Birkett', a reflection of three generations of climbing which started with Jim, who was born in Little Langdale and worked as a slate river in the local quarry.

The flow of climbers into the Lakes was one expression of the appetite for 'wild' places that continued to grow in the early decades of the twentieth century. The physical and moral benefits of getting outdoors had been argued for by social improvers from the later nineteenth century onwards. Ruskin himself had been vocal on the subject, though he was rather less impressed when trains brought waves of people into the Lakes who, in his view, lacked the proper moral perspective. By the early twentieth century and particularly after the First World War, people were organising themselves. There was an explosion of groups with diverse and sometimes even contradictory interests in the countryside. Like youth hostelling and cycling, climbing drew people from a variety of towns and backgrounds, enjoying a strong popularity amongst those who spent the bulk of their time in the pits near the coast and in factories elsewhere. Close-knit groups from the same shift and larger outings coordinated by organisations like the 'Workers Sports Federation'. What began largely as an elite extension of the Romantic cult of the mountains was opened up to men and women from other classes, a shift that was local at first, then broader as the cost of transport dropped. Weekends and holidays. A chance of clean air and of responsibility for oneself, free of obligation to the clock or to the shift. For many, the right to scramble and to roam was a basic right of citizenship.[3] Like those other pursuits, visits to the Lakes for climbing fed campaigns for access that challenged the exclusive claims of large estates, helping lay the foundations for the National Park.[4]

> *. . . there is nothing for the hands but a series of shaky plaques with half-inch tops, like slates on an aging roof. All along I can see my fear barrier getting nearer: a soaking stripe as shiny black as liquorice. At its verge I balance on twin thorns of rock and stare across the 'barrier' at a wet but level ledge beyond it that has become my goal. What's the stepping stone? Only a rim four inches long and less than an inch broad, barely tilted inwards. The joint under the eave, previously closed, has relented slightly. I stick my fingerends in, palm upwards, and brace my knuckles downwards against the glacis. The tiny rim has become the hinge of my world . . . I lean along, my right foot edges on the mini-hold, my left foot smears on the slick black slate, my hands tense, my right foot goes for the good step, my left touches the mini hold, thanks it briefly, and then I'm reaching for some semi-detached flakes on the edge of the earth filled gully while elation brims and soaks through me like sunlight . . .*[5]

The diversity of climbing literature is extraordinary but not surprising. Attitudes and motivations amongst climbers are themselves remarkably varied. You get a flavour of this in the names of routes; from the political and the poetic to the personal, crude and the chemically inspired.[6] What is common is the sense that climbing involves much if not all of the self. Though the intensity of the experience depends on where you are, it can occupy mind and body to the full, a close focus that is felt as much as seen. It can also be read upon the body. The marks of old falls and the shape of a forearm; the way that fingers flex when a pinch or a jam is being described. Something similar happens when you work with stone in other ways. The engagement can be just as strong; it can find you. A relationship begins, a two way thing; the line between hand and material losing some of its sharpness. Scales shift in unexpected ways. And as with climbing, the skills that come from a commitment to the work have effects upon the body. Not just the scars of service, but the way it falls into certain shapes; the way a hammer falls without thinking in just the right place.

STONEWORK

Getting blades required a journey. When a certain age was reached or when the time and company was right. It meant taking particular trails, encounters with places and with stories. Orientation to past and present. Tools were needed, and perhaps some blades to exchange. There was ground to be maintained and coppice to be set, obligations discharged in the opening of new

clearings or the building of a lodge. But edges would last beyond immediate need, and in that duration was biography. Names to be recalled when some blades were handed on. That was why their getting mattered.

Stone getting around the Langdales was an episodic event, undertaken when conditions and company required. Embedded in cycles that saw stock taken to the high pastures of late summer, a visit gave a potential for separation, for narratives tied to the journey and the climb. Old clearings, trails walked by earlier generations; signs of the spirits who had made the land. Once there, elevation and the drama of certain routes added to proceedings, to what it meant to participate. Crags that held the actions of ancestral forces in their form. The tops also provided an extraordinary vantage above the trees. Our obsession with summits and flag planting may be a relatively recent invention and not one shared by all. But when conditions allowed, elevation gave a chance to look back along the route and across to other dales, even to the sea. Other valleys and different people, the times and places of life caught in a gesture as the young were instructed by the old.

Approaching the hornstone from many directions, the climb from valley floors brings you up to more gently sloping grass-covered saddles and what is now open moorland. These can also be reached by higher routes, so that the last part of the approach is more or less on the level. Easier on the legs before the final scramble. Still some way below the hornstone itself, these saddles are bisected by the becks and ghylls that walkers still use today for orientation. The scars of desire lines and established footpaths often run in parallel with the water. In a few places, where paths have cut through grass and peat, there are traces of stoneworking. Flakes and angular fragments of tuff bleached by acid soils, some so heavily rotted that they crush to a grey-white paste beneath the boot or between the fingers. These scatters flank the Langdales: near Stake Beck and Thunacarr Knott to the north, on the edges of Stickle Tarn, beneath Harrison Pike and Thorn Crag. Others occur on Brown Tongue above Lingmell Ghyll, on the western approach to Scafell Pike. More still lie concealed by the turf that draws the Herdwicks up each year.

These scatters lie beyond the known extent of hornstone and are the remnants of temporary camps established in the area. Peat had not then spread its mantle across the uplands and conditions were varied. Places above the treeline where stock could graze and where water was never too far, stations on preferred routes in and out. The forest edge below was not too distant, and with it, the promise of game attracted to the browse that could be had amongst the scrub. There was even a small amount of workable stone in the glacial drift that left hummocks on some hillsides. It was to these sorts of settings that people came with their stock, establishing hearths and shelters from which they could make the short walk and the final climb to the stone. And it was often to these camps that they brought it back; angular blocks to be split and worked into roughouts. The percussive sound of flaking accompanying talk around the fire, curses when one end of a roughout parted company with the other. Some camps were probably used many times. A return meant tracing the outline of earlier visits in heaps of flaking debris, just as walkers use piecemeal cairns to keep them on the way. Platforms cleared, hearths cleaned out and relit, the recent past brought to the surface with the ash.

The wide distribution of these camps is a sign of different customary routes, a variety to the people who recognised a connection with the source. There were times when camps on a particular saddle gave vantage across to others, people moving between them to renew old ties and reach agreement on how working would proceed. The sharing of food harvested from the forest on the way, an animal slaughtered to celebrate a successful trip. News, gossip and plans for the coming year. In the scattered social landscapes of the time, the hornstone was a time and a place where encounters could be anticipated. Some trips may have even been preceded by meetings around lowland hearths, access sanctioned before feet and hooves could take the trail. Bonds with distant kin or those seldom seen came into focus here. In trade, in agreements on a marriage and in the to and fro of talk. Above all else (in every sense), they could be realised through working, through labouring together in arrangements that broke with much of day-to-day experience. Visited in this way, the source possessed many of the qualities of a monument.

> *. . . it started for me with hostelling in the fifties. There was always a gang of us and though we ended up all over the place, it just seemed like a good thing to do every Easter . . . you know . . . to catch up, get together . . . it's strange to think that's half a century ago, some of it's like yesterday . . . we sometimes joke about who'll scatter the last pot . . . We're not so nimble either, but it still helps to get in touch . . . you know . . . with each other and with what's important . . . it's like stepping out of things and stepping back a bit . . .*

This variety is reflected in another way that is easily missed. The more time you spend along the outcrop, the more you get your eye in. The shapes of flakes and quarry-fractured stone, the colour of fresh exposures and more weathered scars and screes. Every so often, the eye fastens upon something unusual. A different colour or texture, a different form. Lying on the surface are some of the stone hammers used during the Neolithic. Left in anticipation of a return, they now lie idle. Most are fairly large; mauls used in the quarrying of the parent stone and the preliminary splitting of blocks. The size of a volleyball, they required both hands when working a face, bodies twisting from the waist with each blow delivered. Fashioned by the becks and rivers from which they were collected, these rounded and abraded cobbles were carried up to particular working areas and left behind. A counterbalance for the roughouts that were taken down. The return to a particular quarry meant a return to

The Langdales

these tools, lifting them from old flaking floors, and from ledges where they had been cached. Picking up where you or those before you had left off.

We cannot say precisely which rivers or becks these cobbles were rescued from. Some are coarse tuffs and others granite, all stones found within the central fells and scattered by the ice. However, the variety used again suggests approaches along more than one route. With smaller hammers, the picture is less clear. There are few that fit in the hand so that fingers can curl and grip during more careful forms of flaking, where a maul would be a sledgehammer on a nut. These are, of course, more difficult to spot, and it may also be that the final stages of flaking were sometimes undertaken with tools of antler or dense wood that have not survived. But smaller stones probably travelled back and forth with people, never far from the hand. It takes time to find the right weight and balance in a hammerstone, to keep just the right face for flaking. The weight has to work with and not against the action. Perhaps they too became attached to people, discarded only when a split or loss of mass prevented further effective use.

> . . . *You can bend slate you know. Only when its fresh; but you can bend the crack when you're riving, keep it regular when you know how it works. . . The trick is not to think about it* . . .

So what of the work itself? How was hornstone extracted and working organised from face to flaking floor? Here again, the picture is complicated; the source is extensive and the deposits varied. So too was working. Some of the smallest sites are no more than tests; single episodes and single axes, people trying out the stone and finding it wanting in some way. The angle of bedding and the consistency vary so much that in some areas it was effectively unworkable. Other sites were only worked a handful of times, and this left small quantities of debris scattered across the fellsides. It was those parts of the outcrop to which people returned over many generations that have the strongest signa-

In the cloud, it gets turned round, the rest goes and you're nowhere

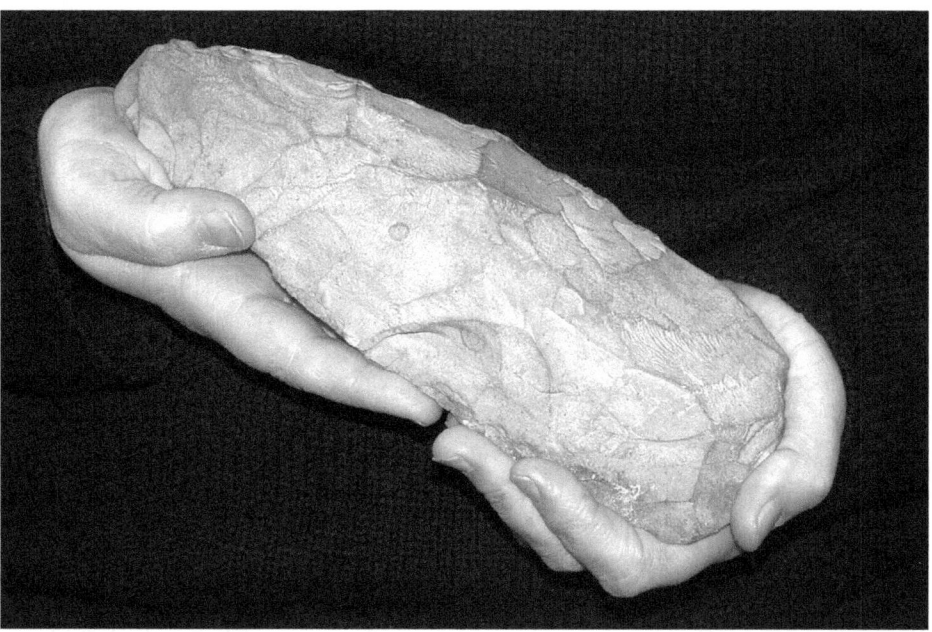

tures; the greatest densities of material and the widest range of evidence for the character of working. The greatest concentrations of these occur around the Langdales, deposits so dramatic that it is easy to see why terms such as 'axe factory' were once coined to describe them.

Though not industrial as we understand it, work was nonetheless specialised and skilful. It brought together techniques that were familiar in other fields and knowledge that was specific to the place. It took time to learn. And it involved a relationship with the stone that was intimate indeed, one in which the rock played an active part. It lent itself to particular ways of working and resisted others, stubborn and even dangerous when approached the wrong way. On fellsides below the outcrop, people scrambled amongst the scrub and tree cover, the knuckles of rowan, thorn and oak clinging to the scree that broke through the coarse grass. They tapped the stone, listening for its consistency. Like a bell in a foundry, good stone rings true. Suitable pieces were worked on the spot or carried off for flaking elsewhere. Scatters of flakes are thin, suggesting a relatively ad hoc and piecemeal pattern to work: an axe here and an axe there. Short episodes undertaken as people collected firewood for their hearths or to use on higher quarries.

On the blockfields below Harrison Stickle, near Glaramara, or on the flanks of Scafell Pike, stone had also taken leave of its parent. Ice had flexed inside creaking joints and had fractured the stone into blocks, heaving these into angular and broken fields below the crags. Much of the working around Scafell exploited these conditions. Where slopes were steeper, blocks had tumbled with the thaw and settled in downslope, some larger than a Herdwick, some

The Langdales

no longer than a hand. These too were a focus for working; small groups levering their way through the weathered topstone and exposing fresher material below. Flaking would then take place within the hollows created by the ring of upcast, the echoes of hammering and the clatter of flakes as they fell to the ground. Lichen stained and weathered now, scars can still be traced on some of the blocks. Stone was also tested and roughouts begun before being carried back to camps for final flaking. There was no single way of doing things, and here again, though work probably required cooperation, the scale of the endeavour was often small.

Similar patterns of working were inscribed on several buttresses around Langdale, and particularly near the head of Dungeon Ghyll. Here, on a ridge that runs out towards Thorn Crag, stone was won by working down onto the top of the outcrop. When the light is right or the last snows linger, it is still possible to trace a series of irregular hollows along the flat, a remnant of open-cast working and of digging down into the loose and fractured rock. Here, as on the blockfields around Scafell, wooden levers may have been brought to help in the opening up of fractures; poles and wedges cut and fire hardened in anticipation before the final climb. Debris from extraction and from working can be seen where it spills down the steep sides of the ghyll. There has also been more recent digging here. Excavation revealed that working in the area

Opposite *I know we're on the right line as we scramble round to the pinnacle*

took the form of a sequence; episodes of extraction separated by intervals long enough for the ground to have healed over before people returned.

In a place where history and myth overlapped, it is impossible to know how people regarded the features they encountered. Old flaking floors and quarry hollows may have been remembered and associated with particular times and people. Some were passed without remark, the upcast no more than a guide to the possibility of good stone nearby. Perhaps the blockfields themselves were regarded as ancient flaking floors, the debris of working by the first people or even spirits. To work such places was to be in step with tradition, to pay respect to collective memory in the process. Where our common sense tends towards the practical, theirs may have slanted things differently.

> *. . . Be careful. The rock, which seems dead, instead is full of deception. Sometimes it changes its nature even while you're digging . . .*

These patterns are difficult to read, and it makes little sense to trace in them a standardised industry or approach. There was the testing of stone and a blade when the opportunity arose, a forerunner to the tap of the geologist's hammer though to rather different ends. Getting to know the stone and its potentials along the outcrop. There was also the return to established areas, a sense of an order to things, of recognised, even named locations that could be described while still on the trail. A local history recalled as people fell into customary ways of turning over a blockfield. Work involved several hands and levers, a tight knot of people. Perhaps close kin, or the members of different lines, bound together in raising overburden and working in a hollow. There is also a variety in the roughouts themselves, some made on the spot or finished off in company near the warmth of a hearth before being carried down at the end of a visit. Crude and asymmetrical forms that would need a lot of grinding; finer roughouts with the finished line already clear. Some as long as a forearm, others more diminutive; even slender, parallel-sided pieces. Though we only find the rejects at the source, there are strong hints of differences in the intended size and form of finished blades and in the level of skill or know-how realised in flaking.

The stone was not easy to work, particularly when it presented itself as angular blocks. It took time to learn how to split them, to bring a rough symmetry to blanks and to reduce the mass while controlling form. Though time spent working flint would have helped, the properties of the hornstone were not identical. Get the angle too steep or the blow too far in and the roughout could snap. Hinge a thick flake from the surface and add many hours to the grinding. It was easy to take a bad path through the stone, to lose the shape or carry on when it was better to stop. Familiarity took practise, observation and instruction, and skills were a common current in talk as people sat or squatted around their camps. You can see it in the roughouts – products of

confident hands alongside those still finding their way, each reject a stepping stone. And always, talk wandered into other areas. Learning how to work meant learning why the axe was important and many other things besides. Skills are always social. Perhaps that mattered as much as any particular blade; learning to talk and to recognise good work meant learning about one's place in the company and in the broader world. Skills acquired near the crags marked people out after their return to lodges in the lowlands.

ON THE EDGE

There are certain settings where skills came together in a more dramatic way. In elevated locations that are often difficult to reach, are signs of more consistent quarrying. Flake scars can be found all over the crags along the band of hornstone, some a product of hammering, others the bounce of a rockfall. In places, these scars overlap and concentrate on near-vertical faces that have been consistently and carefully worked to detach large blocks and massive flakes. Where exposed through the rough mat of bilberry and heather, these faces have aprons of scree containing thousands of flakes, quarrying debris and abraded hammers. Other benches lie concealed by the vegetation or by screes that emanate from working faces further up the outcrop. There are also hollows and small caves, natural fissures in the rock and these too show signs of working – flake scars around their mouths and deposits within. Many of these quarries are perched on the narrow ledges and benches that give the buttresses their steep and stepped profile. Many are also highly vulnerable to erosion, mobile when walked upon and all too easily disturbed. Excavation suggests that some of them developed during the earlier third millennium, sometime after the source was first exploited.

These quarries give a remarkable picture of working, but there are puzzles here as well. The approach to many involved a sharp scramble and exposure to perilous drops. Settings were tricky to reach and sometimes even dangerous. Yet good stone for working was available on far more easily accessed crags and this was not always worked. Just why this happened is not altogether clear. Some places may have simply been overlooked. But again, there was more to it than that. The spread of quarries suggests that exposure to risk was sometimes part of the process, adding to the act and the axes that were made. Going 'out on a limb' to remote and dangerous locations was a deliberate choice. It marked a sharp threshold to be crossed by those who knew where the quarries were, a withdrawal, out of sight from others back at camp or on the upland plateau. And when the cloud came down, as it often did, mist rolling off the plateau to hide the crags, the world itself withdrew from view. There was a potential for separation here that lent working some of the qualities of a ritual.

> *. . . Sometimes after work I'll walk up from the house and behind Raw Pike towards the tarn…there's spots I always stop at on the way . . . for a good half hour I won't see anyone, but as you drop back down you can see and hear them clear enough . . . all over the stone and by the water . . . even saw someone windsurfing last year, he'd lugged it all the way up . . . I like it more when it's quiet but I don't own it . . . anyway you never know who you're going to meet . . .*

Other lines were also drawn. The face of the mountain was broken up by the sharp faults and folds of buttresses, benches, ledges and layers and these 'breaks' define the limits of many quarries. There are certainly paths of least resistance here. But in these responses to the prevailing pattern of the crags, there are hints of distinctions being drawn. Close links between particular groups and specific parts of the outcrop, quarries tied to particular kin, other faces to other lines. The source as a whole brought people together, but lines could be more closely drawn and traced in the stone itself. In an area where even today individual crags are known and named places, it would take special pleading to suggest that associations at the time were not equally close and personal.

What did work involve? We know that people brought timber with them, boughs of oak and brushwood which were used to set fires against bench and crag. These cracked and weakened the stone which was then detached as blocks. Fire also helped to create sharp edges and overhangs on the face and these were worked directly to detach large flakes. For those making their way in around Bow Fell or through Langdale Combe, the smoke from these remote crags was a sign that others were already in place. Several quarries may have been open at the same time, and where this happened, there was the possibility of help needed in firing and quarrying, for observation and for talk as some climbed to work near others.

Fire setting was not easy. Temperature and duration had to be right; too little and there was no change; too much and the stone became cracked and crazed. You had to know the properties of wood from different trees, what thicknesses were best and how to stack it. Timber had to be chosen and collected, the first stage of work before the crags were even reached. Once there, the clearing of debris and the setting of the fire introduced a real drama to proceedings. Beyond the fire itself, the heat had many effects on the rock. As temperatures rose, cracks would begin to open with a snap, trapped water would be released with a hiss or sigh. The stone would cough, groan and shift; it could splinter violently in unpredictable ways. Sudden rockfalls or shards that sprang from the face and caused injury if you stood too close. It would be easy to trace a sense of animation in sound and movement, to conclude that the stone was somehow alive and a partner in the process.

Once detached by fire and hammer, the stone was worked *in situ*, roughouts completed on or near the quarry faces. There was skilful and considered working here to match the careful use of fire. A confidence in flaking and a regularity of finish on many roughouts not seen everywhere. There are cruder forms too, the products of less-accustomed hands; a signal once again of a younger presence alongside those with more experience. Induction, observation, instruction. Where to place the first strike – what to hear behind the fire – how to turn an edge and hold a line. Work in view of others, making the technical familiar, words and actions second nature. For those who were still learning, the thin and well-trimmed waste flakes on many quarries suggest that there were good lessons to be learnt from watching others bring elegant roughouts from the rock. They could even hear it; in the ring of flakes and the rhythm of striking. And after flaking, a return to the face, mauls raised to detach more stone. Blocks picked over at the base of the crag and moved to one side for further work. Pauses to relieve the sharp ache between the shoulders, close cooperation with others before the focus pulled down once more to the roughout in the hand. Sequences suggest cycles repeated several times, ledges worked back to steepen the incline, spoil slipping down to bury older quarries below.

Just how long each episode lasted we cannot say. A month or so, probably no more than that. There were always other matters to attend to and the volume of production may not have been the pressing concern. There was enough. It was time to return to the cattle and the camps, to anticipate a descent to lower ground. There would be another time. The evidence was all around you, in forgotten and familiar hammers, and in screes or scars so old that they had always been there. Whether other tokens were left to mark the close we cannot say. This happened at other sources, suggesting that outcrops were sometimes places that received as well as gave. Who knows what lies beneath the surface?

Maintained in the shadow of scarred crags, customary ways of working brought the past into the present. There was history here, once you knew how to read it. Of earlier generations and different lines, of older ties and origin myths that bound those lines together. As work drew people up across the generations, crags had new names inscribed across older associations. Kin who had worked years before; faces that had been argued over, perhaps even deaths when the stone bit back. These added to tradition and to the event itself, to what it meant to participate in quarrying and flaking alongside others. In a world where this stone mattered, there were also times when access broke with customary patterns and became a source of tension, the rights of some contested by others. To work was to become accustomed to the stories of the stone.

When the time came to leave, for knots to unravel into different threads, the people who scattered along different paths took many things with them. There were the roughouts themselves, carried in bags and perhaps across the

shoulders of animals. Many had been flaked to their full extent, others required more work before grinding and polishing could commence. These were all tasks for the future, something to anticipate on the journey to more familiar ground. And where working had brought several lines together, there was also the news that had been passed, the talk of lives that wound through different valleys and along more distant stretches of the coast. This would have a currency on return, and agreements made at the source would have implications for the life of the community in the coming seasons.

People took other things as well. Stone getting was a physical activity, it had effects upon the body and these persisted after leaving the source. Cuts and other injuries sustained during quarrying or flaking; a tightening of the breath from the dust. As years passed, repeated visits to the source lay down more sediment, a rattle in the chest that could not be shaken off. The signs of participation were there for others to see and hear. There were other signs too. It could be heard in the talk of those who had made the journey for the first time; their knowledge of the outcrop and of stoneworking itself. And it could be read in their bodies, in the ways that they brought a hammer to stone, in the familiarity of their gestures and coordination. Skills took time to polish, but they were on the path.

CHAPTER 7

TRUTH TO MATERIAL

> *. . . It is difficult to describe in words the meaning of forms because it is precisely this emotion which is conveyed by sculpture alone. Our sense of touch is a fundamental sensibility . . .*[1]

The quarries were silent, at least for a time. Mauls settled into working floors or perched on ledges, waiting to be raised again. Invisible before, foxes scavenged hesitantly amongst midden. Hearths grew cold. Struck camps behind them, people and cattle scattered like erratics, retracing their steps along ridges and down through darker dales. A weight on the hoof and across the shoulder, the stone they carried was an expectation, the possibility of a blade.

Well-made roughouts could have been used as they were, as wedges and as tools for digging. You could have even got away with grinding just the cutting edge where skilful flaking had left a smooth enough surface over the body. However, this was not a common practice. After the journey and the scramble, the time spent at the face, it mattered that task and stone were taken to a more distinctive conclusion. This generally happened in low-lying areas where more persistent traditions of settlement could be traced. Beyond the source, roughouts have been identified in Lower Furness, further up the coast and across the Solway Plain, where they turn up as stray finds or in association with scatters of flintwork. Some have also been found around Keswick and Ambleside, their recovery a reflection of the pace of tourism. More villas and hotels meant more digging. Others turn up at various points along the Eden Valley and further to the north.[2]

In these chance recoveries, we see a trace of people returning with the good stone. After time away, those who had made the journey returned to their lodges. With them were fattened stock and perhaps some game they had taken on the way; news of those from other valleys who had parted company further up the trail. Stories to exchange in return for accounts of whom or what had passed in their absence. Where return coincided with the autumn, arrival swelled the company available for the harvest; of crops and of the forest. Labour to lay in stores and set things straight before winter took hold and the land died back.

Roughouts fashioned in one company were now transformed in another. Grinding was very different from flaking. In familiar hands, a roughout could be brought from a blank in half an hour so, a little more if there were problems. It involved a good deal of turning and checking, even a change or two in the hammers that were used. But once started, the work dropped into a rhythm and often did not stop until a form was realised. That is, of course, when it didn't go wrong, or when the task was sidetracked by the talk. Grinding on the other hand took hours, even days, and was more easily broken up into episodes; worked around other tasks. It also involved a different sort of persuasion. Each time a hammer struck, the stone had options; to take the anticipated path or to break in unexpected ways, even to remain as it was. Grinding was

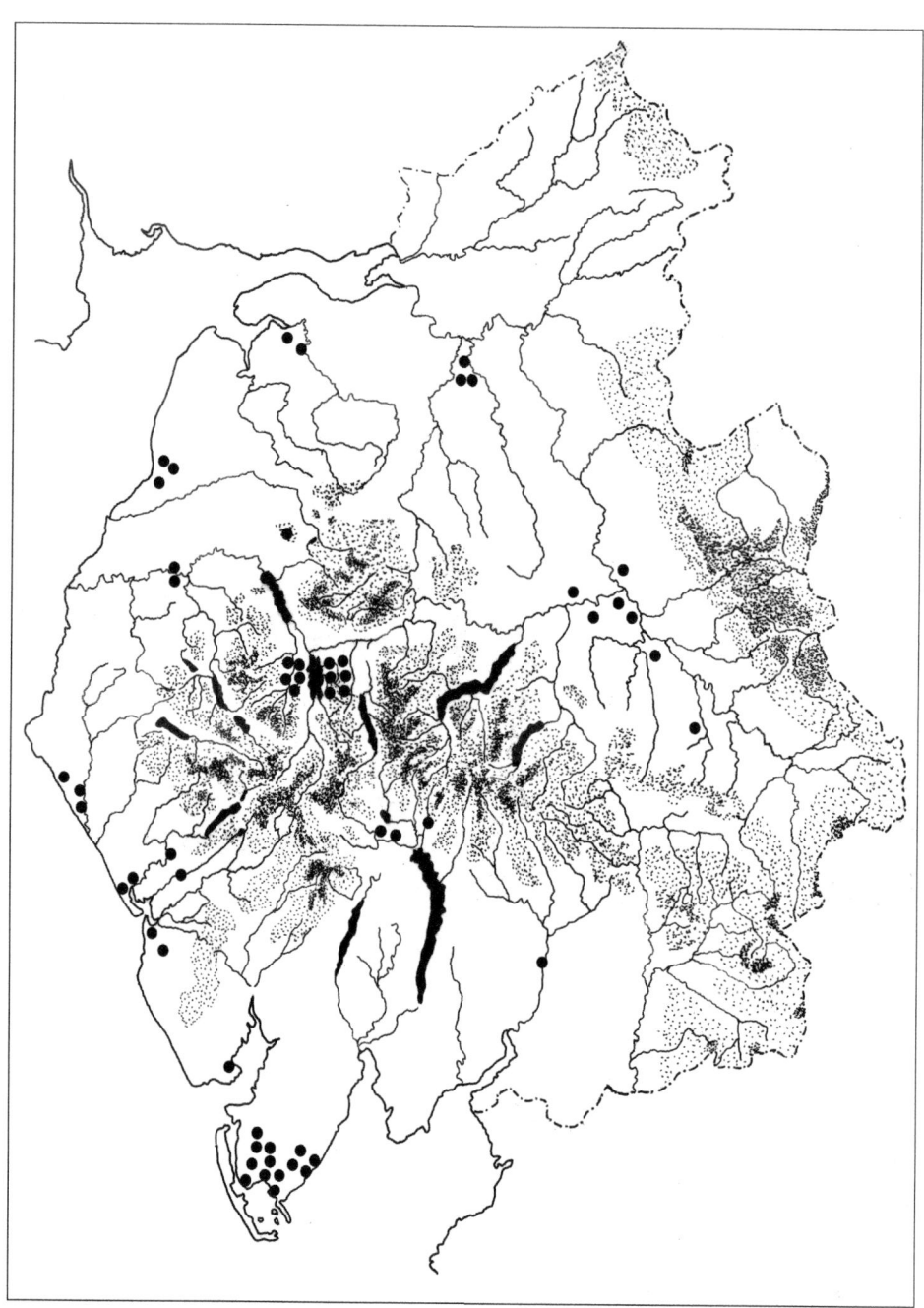

The distribution of roughout axes of Cumbrian stone

patient. Like ice, it worked more slowly and this allowed a more intimate, less risky level of control over form. For the ridges and hollows of the roughout it was only a matter of time.

It involved a harsh surface at first; a block of grit or granite across which the roughout was pushed and pulled. Often used for extended periods, these polissoirs eventually acquired dished and polished surfaces which would also be used when a cutting edge needed to be reset. It also required water; the stone became thirsty during grinding and a trickle helped maintain an abrasive paste. Other tools were also used, hand held rubbers of fine grained sandstone that, like larger polissoirs, have turned up on excavated sites and in more fragmented scatters. Such work was not unusual. It bore more than a passing resemblance to the grinding of flour on querns, the blocks used for each task looking rather similar. Shoulders over the stone, a steady motion back and forth; water and sand added from time to time rather than grain.

Cumbria has very few excavated Neolithic sites. Ehenside Tarn is one of the best and even that is poorly understood. That makes it difficult to determine how activities like grinding and polishing were caught up in the flow of life. The fact that rubbers and polissoirs turn up in association with broader spreads of flint does, however, suggest that finishing was a familiar sight on many settlements at the time. After all, these were places where water was generally ready to hand and where time itself was often available. And if a task took someone up the trail, a roughout and a rubber could make the journey with them.

There was probably no standard requirement that all of the roughouts brought back from the source had to be ground at once. This is suggested by the fact that in the few cases where groups of implements have been recovered, they often include both roughouts and ground examples. A few may have been propped against the side of the lodge or cached out of the way for grinding when the need arose. When an existing blade broke beyond the possibility of repair, or when several were needed for some form of exchange. The nature of that need may have also influenced the forms that were realised, the shape and finish of individual blades. The setting was important though. It meant that the final stages of making often happened where there was an audience of sorts; those who lived and worked close by. On the edge of the settlement or around the evening fire. Where the task involved finishing a token as well as a tool, the connection with the maker was made all the more familiar by the fact that it was witnessed. And because it was a familiar part of life around the lodge, there was always the chance for children to gain a casual apprenticeship through observation and mimicry. To get in the way while work progressed, or to practise on discarded stone.

> *. . . you can see the changes, but when it's rough, even when it's cut, it looks a lot the same . . . it gets greyer and powdery so you can't really tell . . . the polishing though, that's when the colour comes back, and all the patterns . . .*

The connection was even closer for the ones who put their weight onto the polissoir. Even here there was skill to be developed, a discipline of the body to be acquired. A technique of persuasion. Knowing when to switch from one face to the other; how to check the line along the side and how to finish the cutting edge. Patience too; these things took time and it helped if there was a pattern to the work. One cannot always tell. Some blades have been worked to a finer polish that has removed all traces of the labour. But on close inspection, many retain long facets from grinding that run from the butt to the bevel of the cutting edge. These reveal that grinding often progressed in a sequence; hands pressed down and maintained at certain angles for a period, the angle changed only when a sharp and flattened surface had been achieved. Balance then shifted to create another, the pattern repeated on both faces. After this was done, weight switched towards the ridges between the facets, slowly bringing them down to a smooth and continuous surface. As roughout gradually turned to blade, the steady rhythm of grinding would be broken by pauses; a hand to wipe the paste from the face, the stone raised to the eye. A flattened palm across the surface, feeling for dips and growing accustomed in the process. Recognition growing stronger each time.

Levels of finish tend to vary. There are many where a shallow flake scar can still be traced on the surface, often to one side and away from the cutting edge. Scars can also be seen on blades reworked and maintained during use, their edges sharpened and reduced by regrinding. Yet there are also many where all traces of the earlier stages in the task have been completely erased. On these, grinding was sometimes followed by polishing, a process involving fine sand or silt and water rubbed up and down the blade by hand. The hornstone could take a very definite shine when this was done and the final stages of grinding and polishing seem to have been as much about bringing out colour and lustre as anything else. How clear was the colour, how sharp was the line. Finishing was often as much a matter of aesthetics as it was of utility.

This extended to the hafts in which most were set. These are rare, but when found, they offer a glimpse of a subtle and complex process of judgement. To begin with there was the wood itself. Several species had potential, amongst them ash, beech and oak. Shape and the orientation of the grain were also important. The blanks for hafts were often cut from the lower portion of large trees, the bend where the trunk met the roots retained to serve as the broader end where the hollow for the blade was cut and gouged. This was the case with the beech wood haft, recovered with blade in place, from Ehenside Tarn. Work involved axes and wedges, tools already hafted for the task. Some hafts were probably cut from managed woodland, where material with the right combination of taper, flexibility and potential toughness could be harvested. Where this happened, the wood itself had a

Opposite *Limestone underfoot, the Pikes on the skyline*

The Langdales

Grinding slab from Ehenside Tarn. Darbishire 1873. Society of Antiquaries of London

history, a connection with people. Selection and cutting took time to learn, lessons when a blank was cut too thinly or against the best of the grain. Fresh hardwoods were easier to work; timber toppled years before could be as stubborn as stone; a balance in choice was necessary. Hafts required a knowledge of materials and a sensitivity in their treatment that took years to acquire, a skill practised and polished at the coppice stool and in the splitting of planks. On the shoulder or in the hand, the form and quality of the haft was as important as the blade itself.

> *. . . The whole surface has been most carefully cut by repeated blows of a cutting instrument, showing cuts and ridges an eighth of an inch apart in small concave facets. Between the celt and the hand these are arranged in a spiral manner round the wood, perhaps while turning the wood in the hand during the process of finishing. The boat-shaped head of this haft has been accurately ground across the grain in several facets as truly as any modern joiner could cut it with his sharpest chisel. The whole is a beautiful specimen of the skill and finish of the ancient workman. The chipped dressing of the surface is so neat that one cannot avoid detecting in it a certain idea of ornamentation . . .*[3]

Once cut, the blank required shaping; the thicker end rounded or swept back behind the line of the handle. This could then be hollowed out to receive the blade, a task achieved with smaller blades or chisels and with flakes of flint to adjust the angle and tightness of the fit. There was judgement here as well; a badly-mounted or ill-used blade would act as a wedge and split the haft in two. Familiarity with tolerance was essential and once the appropriate shape had been achieved, the haft would be left to dry or toughened on a spent fire, perhaps even decorated by carving or by superficial charring. The fit had to be right and so did the angle. Eighty to ninety degrees or thereabouts where felling was intended; sharper angles for carpentry and lopping. The angle of cutting edges shows that some were also hafted flat as adzes, useful for many tasks including hafting itself.

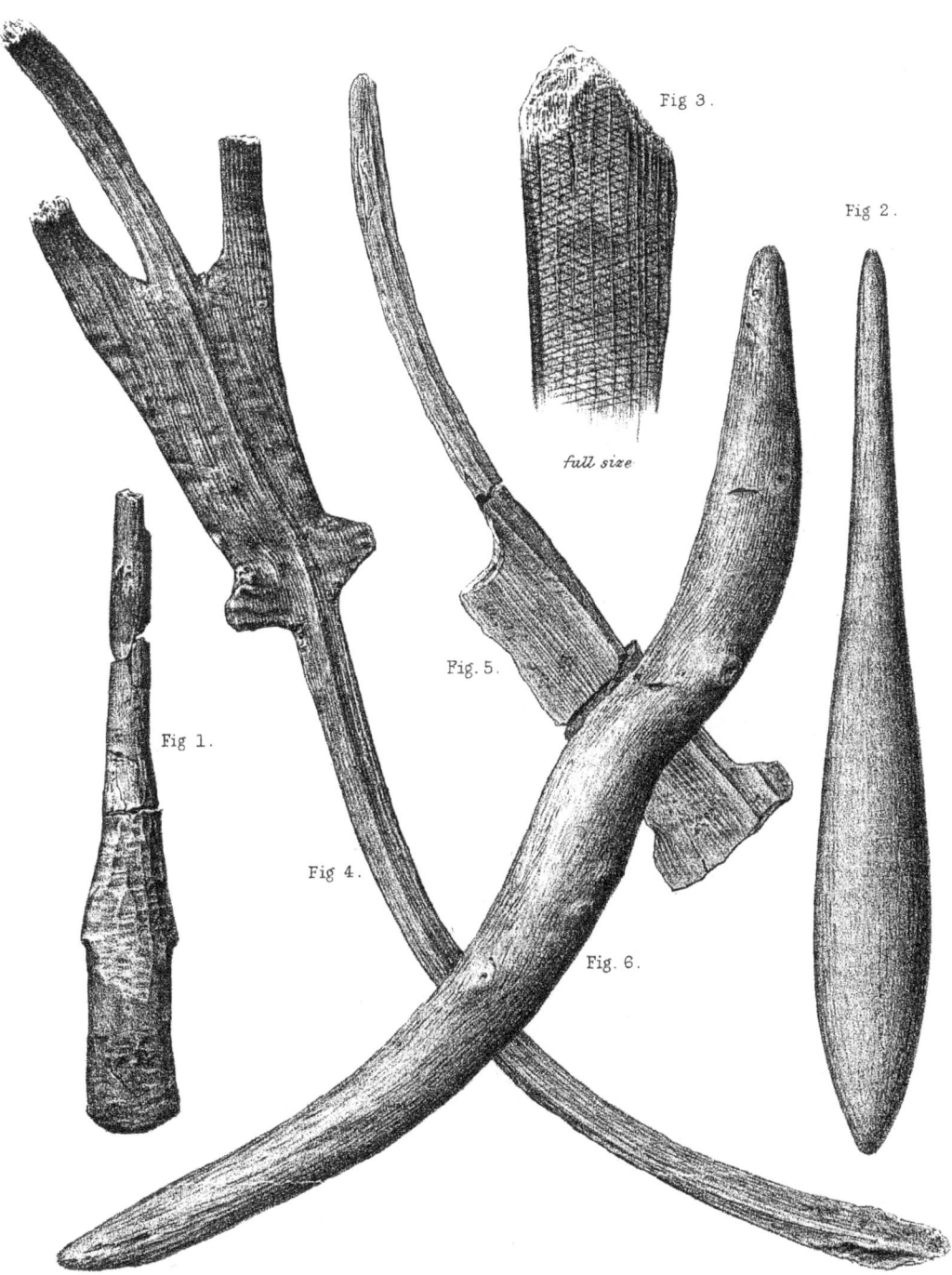

Wooden implements recovered from Ehenside Tarn; an axe haft appears bottom left in the engraving. Darbishire 1873.
Society of Antiquaries of London

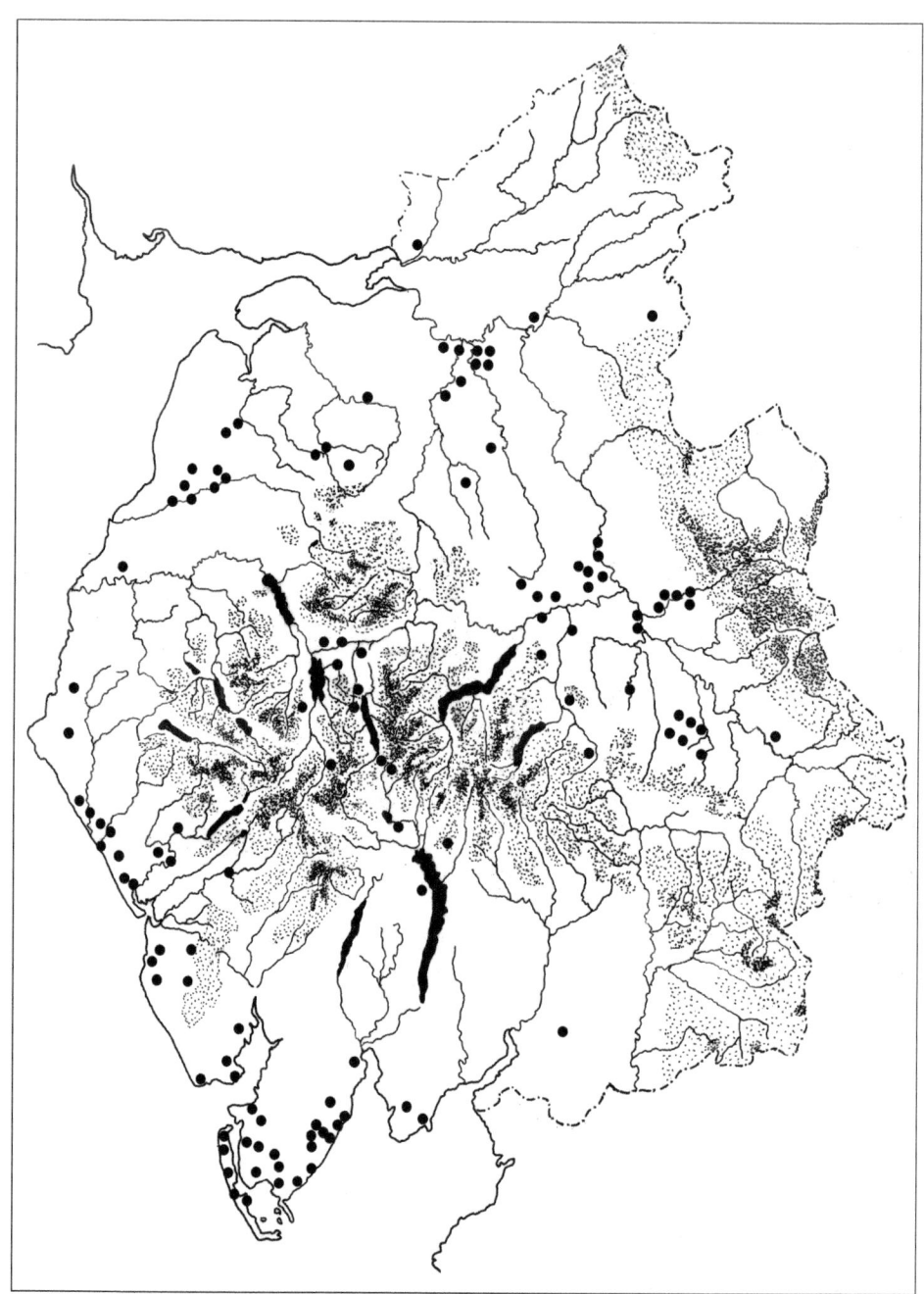

The distribution of ground and/or polished axes of Cumbrian stone

As with grinding, the process involved pauses; checking the hafting hollow, inserting the blade and raising the tool to look along the line. An assessment of balance and ease in the hand. Was the weight distributed so that the tool did its share of the work? Would it hang comfortably over the shoulder? Did it look right? Our sample of hafts is too small to take the argument very far, but it may be that styles of hafting and binding were sometimes sensitive to identity. The appearance of hafts said something about the origins and affiliations of those who carried and used them, skill in their making a source of local respect.

> . . . it wasn't that long after I'd started in the workshop. I'd been working on this carving for a week or so, a relief in oak . . . I'd left my bag at home and so I picked up one of Mick's gouges and started using it. I wasn't used to it but it was better than nothing. Anyway, Mick came in and took it straight out of my hand, gave me a right mouthful . . .

Many blades were probably hafted more than once. A habit to be acquired, good use could mean a long life. This meant knowing how best to set and use them and about the materials that you worked. How heartwood was tougher than the sapwood beneath the bark, how bone was best split to get marrow free of splinters. Edges would need attention from time to time, sharpened or repaired where small flakes flew off during use; a misdirected blow or a knot in the timber. Even when more serious breaks occurred, blades could be removed and reworked and there are many in collections which show this form of attention. A truncated cutting edge that dips too steeply from the body of the blade; side facets that stop abruptly. These are the hallmarks of tools used and used again, even handed down. Over time, they changed shape and reduced in size, perhaps shifting in their usefulness. What started life as a sharp edge for felling could finish as a tool for finer and more delicate work. It was that way for people too. Years spent polishing the shape of different tasks; the body acquiring scars and changing as you moved through life. The condition and use of a blade was a cue for memory and a metaphor for the journey. Maybe some were the butt of jokes.

The distribution of finished blades across the region is more extensive than that of roughouts. There are more of them too. It also overlaps with more low-lying ground where later Old Norse place names refer more frequently to settlements than to topography. The pattern is by no means clear-cut. Most have been chance finds and opportunities for recovery vary according to terrain and the pattern of more recent land use. But in a region where the landscape is so physically varied, their distribution sketches at least some of the contours of customary traditions of dwelling. Many are probably derived from settlements; associated features passed or cut unrecognised by contractors. Others reflect chance losses on the trail, and a few may have been disturbed from more specialised deposits. These include a number of 'hoards', identified from the later nineteenth century onwards; collections of roughouts and of polished blades from places like Portinscale.[4]

These patterns become more interesting when set alongside the details of form. The source was used by people who came from different valleys and from different sides of the central fells. Blades were finished 'closer to home' and were often maintained over considerable periods of time. Can we see more local traditions of working in the broader spread? The simple answer is probably no. Use and attrition have left their mark on so many blades that it is impossible to determine if ways of working were significantly different from one part of the region to another. And given that the source was in use for fifteen hundred years or more, it would be surprising if the distribution of communities remained in any strong sense static. Shifts of fortune and location, even the reworking of connections through marriage, these create a composite picture rather than a snapshot. Our distanced view is all the more confused because even within Cumbria at the time, blades were moving from one hand and one community to another through exchange. Someone at a gathering in the later fourth millennium would have been able to read a good deal in the character of the blades and hafts that others carried. We cannot.

The picture is confusing, but not entirely without pattern. Many blades take the form that they do because of maintenance and repair. But there are some where we can still get an idea of original and intended forms. The most striking are the blades known as 'Cumbrian Clubs'.[5] Varied in size but usually large, these are highly distinctive, often with a slight waisting towards the butt and flattened facets on either side. Many of the details of this form are repeated on smaller blades as well, and these are often referred to in the literature as 'Cumbrian'. These striking pieces demonstrate that it often wasn't enough to simply finish a tool to meet immediate needs. It had to look right, to conform to certain expectations. A shape that was easily recognised, an attention to the surface that brought out the colour in the stone. This suggests a subtle audience of judgement. Perhaps senior members of the community or others, for whom the form of a blade said something about the maker or the hands through which it would pass. An audience that, real or imagined, looked over your shoulder as you worked. The idea was sometimes there from an early stage. Many of the larger and more finely-flaked roughouts in the area seem to anticipate just such a shape. The result of careful and accustomed working, they demonstrate that sometimes the intended form was already clear as people made the journey to the outcrop.

> *... a small sculpture only 3 or 4 inches big can have about it a monumental scale, so that if you photographed it against a blank wall in which you had nothing to refer it to but only itself – or you photographed it against infinite distance – a small thing only a few inches big, might seem, if it has a monumental scale, to be any size . . .*[6]

Truth to Material

Found across the region, the spread of Cumbrian axes hints at both the circulation of blades and a sense of an accepted form. A sense that went far beyond the immediate horizons of extended families on the plain or in different valleys. The idea was ground into people at the source; by suggestion and by observation of the tools that others carried across their shoulders. It was reground at other times and in other settings too, when people met or gathered; when the form of a blade and what it said about you came into sharper focus. However it was sustained, the simple fact of distribution is a demonstration of a tradition and a sensibility that went well beyond the local.

It would be easy to take this line too far. To evoke a sense of 'design' more appropriate to the present than to the Neolithic and to imply that all blades were expected to look exactly the same. That was not how it was. Beyond the idea that the hornstone was used primarily to make axes, blades *did* vary. Some are more or less trapezoidal, with sharp straight sides that stop abruptly at the cutting edge. Others taper slightly before the head and not all possess distinctive side facets. Even the roughouts found away from the source suggest that people had an expectation of making blades of different shapes and sizes. There

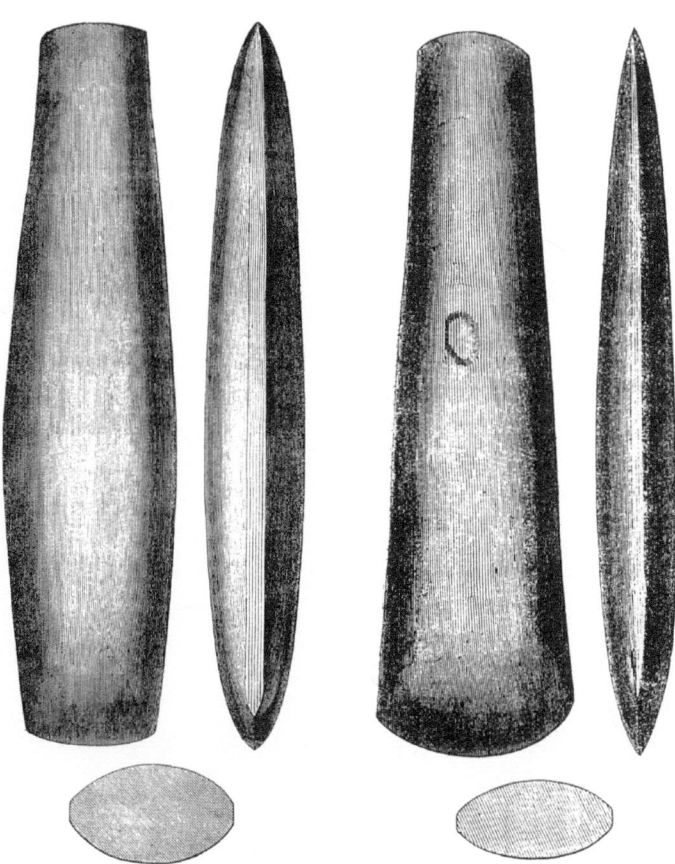

was no singular directive. Form was often a matter of personal choice, a response to what particular pieces of stone allowed. That said, the range is such that it does invite certain questions. Were many of the more distinctive 'Cumbrian Clubs' the result of particular hands and more specialised working? Did people make a variety of blades for use, and more dramatic and distinctive forms for exchange and display?

Perhaps. Large and distinctive 'Cumbrian Clubs' have been found in Ireland and Scotland and across the Pennines, and some of the larger and more distinctive roughouts that formed the basis for these have a close association with quarries around the Langdales. But that association is not exclusive and similar roughouts recovered even further afield cannot be tied to specific parts of the source. They may yet lie undiscovered on Scafell or around Glaramara. They were also being produced over a considerable period and there is as yet no evidence that finishing was focused in any one part of the region. As for making different axes for different purposes, there are many parallels for just such a distinction. A token that was made for use as a gift might have been regarded differently from one which was intended to hang across your shoulder for some time. But once again, the picture is not, and was not, clear-cut. Whatever it looked like, sometimes it was simply the fact that a blade had been carried and used by a particular person that made it an appropriate token for circulation. Exchange was an important motive for working the hornstone and may have gained in importance over the course of the Neolithic. But until there is evidence to the contrary, it is best to conclude that this did not create a more specialised class or community of producers. Skill was significant; it contributed to the way that someone was regarded. It did not set them entirely apart.

The picture is a little clearer from further afield, as things often are, usually because they seem simpler. Hornstone blades have been recovered in Scotland and across the Pennines, in Ireland and on the Isle of Man. Forms tend to vary, a result of long sequences of use. Often all we find are fragments of a cutting edge or a butt. But there are some characteristics that are found, not only on the hornstone, but on blades that were made in these different areas. Side facets are common on flint axes to the east, as they are on porcellanite blades from County Antrim. The butts of many axes from this source were also ground to a facet, as were some from Cumbria. Outside this area, these features are relatively rare. The similarities are not enough to infer standardisation, still less that working was in the hands of a distinct group of specialists. But they do suggest that certain ideas about form were recognised by scattered communities over a vast area. That could only happen because of contact and communication; through the overlapping of people.

GATHERING AND SCATTERING

Appleby horse fair. A handful of days in June when all roads rise to meet each other; when a field becomes a focus and a pivot for the year.

Fair Hill, once Gallows Hill, lies on the edge of things; seen from a car window if noticed at all. But for a while in the summer, perspectives change. The ground shifts; becomes a centre of sorts. Hundreds of families move into the Eden Valley and converge on Fair Hill, setting up stalls and grazing horses brought to race and to trade. Numbers vary, but most years there's been a broad range. Piebalds, Cobs, New Forest, Connemara, Welsh and even Drays; regions of Britain and Ireland mapped out in breeds and measured in hands.

Official history has it that the Fair goes back to the seventeenth century, held first within Appleby itself before being moved to the margins. History also records that the Fair has only rarely been suspended, once because of the plague, and again in 2001 because of foot-and-mouth. Beyond these instances, much is made of the continuity of proceedings, roots traced back to the Middle Ages. Some even claim a more extended genealogy. Tourist talk in bars turns on pre-Christian calendars, Pagan celebrations and dimly remembered or invented gods.

Appleby is an anticipated time and place, a point where paths overlap. Part of a traditional calendar, it requires an acknowledgement of a scale of community beyond the everyday. An acknowledgement worked on physically. Arrival, the sorting of pitches and the setting up of stalls. A face-to-face encounter with families that spend much of their time in other regions; some well known, others less so. For the duration of the Fair, lines draw together; people meet, talk, eat, drink and trade. It is common ground. Things are fluid. The selling of tools, stock and materials to other families, the stalls faced to tourists and people from the town; barter with partners, gift giving and more alienated exchanges. Then there are the horses. Taking mares down to the Eden to wash, running lanes to show form; inspection, talk, racing and gambling. There is close scrutiny, questioning of bloodlines, judgement of condition, haggling and the sealing of deals with the slap of one hand upon another.

It's the pattern at other fairs: the gathering and scattering days at Puck, the flux of people, the relaxation of licence. A press of faces not seen since last year or never before. Sometimes never again. Services and blessings; the veneration of saints. Gossip, gaming and casual indiscretion. And after the haggling, the hard trade and the horseplay. What then? Beyond the 'official' duration of the event, things disentangle piecemeal. Deals and agreements sorted and the market shrinking, families leave along different roads, departure encouraged by tightening attitudes in the town. Some remain for longer, but soon, the field slips out of focus and back to the margins. All that remains is a superficial archaeology and a will to return.

CHAPTER 8

OVERLAPPING WORLDS

A weight of awe not easy to be borne
Fell suddenly upon my spirit, cast
From the dead bosom of the unknown past,
When first I saw that sisterhood forlorn; –
And her, whose strength and stature seemed to scorn
The power of years – pre-eminent and placed
Apart, to overlook the circle vast.
Speak Giant-Mother! tell it to the morn,
While she dispels the cumbrous shades of night;
Let the Moon hear, emerging from a cloud,
When, how and wherefore, rose on British ground
That wondrous Monument, whose mystic round
Forth shadows, some have deemed, to mortal sight
The inviolable god that tames the proud.

The stone around the Langdales drew people up. Visited over many centuries, it became a place of practical pilgrimage, a place where the past bled into the present. Times collapsed, one upon another. Work was initiation, a payment of respect, a chance of meeting others and, of course, of getting raw material. Paths stretched from coast and dale to higher fells, then back again; seasons of silence punctuated by the sharp reports of hammering and the groan and tumble of stone. Generation after generation, the residues of working accumulated, adding to the prominence of the place in social memory. People came and went and among a variety of approaches, some quarries came to be more sharply defined; skilful and considered working realised in large and well-finished roughouts.

The outcrop had its most immediate significance for communities scattered across the western and Solway plains or the lower lands to the south and east of the fells. People who had names for different crags and traced their relations in stories of the stone. Those further afield would have heard of it; some may have seen it. It featured in talk around more distant fires and it is possible that some made even longer journeys. That said, most of the roughouts from the source are found within Cumbria, suggesting that access and working most often operated at a scale no greater than the modern region.

This begs an obvious question, one around which arguments have turned for more than half a century. If use of the source was local, bound perhaps by customary rights of access, why do we find so many blades in the far corners of the country? How and why did they get there? After the Second World War, the work of petrologists led some to suggest a national network to match the scale of distributions. Some accounts went further, suggesting that 'trade' was coordinated by specialised entrepreneurs or middlemen who moved axes in bulk by land and sea and into the hands of farmers in other parts of the country.[1] It seemed that things were not that different from the way that slates left Honister in the early twentieth century.

It is easy to see why such images appeal, but they do no more than hold the past up as a mirror to the present. The distances travelled by many blades are remarkable indeed. But the character of their journey slips between our fingers when we assume that things were so direct and so familiar. The world was different. People recognised themselves as members of many communities, and these cut across one another at different scales. Close kin, a line of descent, the company of women or of men, adults and those not yet initiated. Beyond these were broader companies, ones that are hard to put names to: lineages, clans and, on occasion, still larger federations. These could not be mapped into the sharp and exclusive spaces that we take for granted on a modern atlas of nation states. Boundaries were blurred, life was both small-scale *and* extensive.[2]

In these tangled conditions, one of the ways in which people negotiated a path through life was through the circulation of stock, materials, labour and ideas. These exchanges varied depending on the situation and the people involved; it is this that we often miss. Where worlds overlapped, it is unlikely that all blades circulated in the same way or for the same reasons. Ground and finished on settlements across the region, some changed in significance over the course of their lives and at different stages on their journey. They were tools as well as tokens of identity, and these different qualities slipped in and out of focus. This is not so strange. Whatever else it may mean, the knife from the shop is different when it's given or received as a gift, or when it moves from your parents' cutlery drawer into your own. Things attach themselves to people in different ways. They can carry people with them and this potential was no less important in the Neolithic. If anything, it mattered more.

Some transactions took a form that we might recognise as trade; a handful of blades bartered with people from neighbouring valleys, or from further along the coast. Used well, these were good tools. They had density and potential, and could be easily resharpened when an edge lost a flake. They were also striking, in form and in their grey-green colour, and this too may have been part of their attraction. Even here though, transactions were seldom faceless. Bartering between kin, or between trading partners who shared no line of descent was part of the moral economy of the time. An obligation of blood or of affiliation honoured in the exchange. One of the definitions of a close bond with others was the routine and customary to and fro of goods; food shared; stock crossed; blades passed from one hand to another.

There were also gifts. Because they carried people with them, axe blades were well suited for use in exchanges which created new ties. Gifts are curious things. They never fully leave the donor, and are carried in the object or the act that another receives, so much so that anthropologists talk of transactions that involve 'keeping while giving'.[3] Gifts create a lasting tie when handed on. They can also create debts, obligations to be discharged at a later date and in particular ways. Help with a new clearing; access to pasture, support in a claim on a sacred site. Marriages, affiliations between the men or women of different lines, alliances between families; these ties could be addressed through particular forms of gift giving. And in a world where stock and crops were both inheritance and a legacy to bestow, continuity across the generations was also important, negotiated where blades and other things were handed down. This could happen because blades had names and histories behind them, and it may have helped where the blades themselves were physically distinctive and easily recognised.

> *. . . I'd have liked one of the kids to have taken the farm on, to carry on after us. I used to think I was only looking after it so I could hand it on to them. It's not going to happen though. There's no future in this . . . who wants to live in a museum . . .*

In other situations, identities were yet more sharply defined. Where exchange was a form of strategy, inflicting debt upon another created a relationship of dominance. Where lineage heads or others competed for honour and renown, there were many ways in which standing could be claimed, at least for a time. Having the ear of the dead; control over important rituals, the keeping of strong herds, all of these could be important. But there was also giving food through feasts, or more durable presentations which could influence relationships. In many of these circles, the stories read in stone blades supported the creation of debts and the forging of alliances. It was not always that way.

Long Meg and her Daughters from the air. The larger enclosure can be seen to the right of the stone circle.
Photo: Bob Bewley

Sometimes someone simply needed a new blade and knew when and from whom it could be obtained. But when circumstances were different, that same blade might leave the hand as a gift to another. Things could move in and out of focus, mundane or highly charged and back again, depending on who was involved.

Given this mess of values and relations, it serves little purpose to say that blades from the Langdales were more or less valuable, or that their value increased in some direct way with distance from the hornstone. Some did and some did not. As the fourth millennium gave way to the third, axes from Cumbria and from other sources were certainly drawn upon in these ways, within and beyond the region. Their circulation wove people together and as they made their journey, so some blades built up long biographies. Names were recalled when blades were held aloft or deposited; in graves, in ceremonial enclosures, even in rivers. But between these times, many remained on the shoulder where they did no more than whisper their story. Repaired and reground when the need arose, most were eventually released or lost from their hafts without due ceremony.

It is tempting to conclude that some of these developments encouraged more formal and considered forms of working at the source; that the changing roles of axes prompted production geared to more ceremonial forms of exchange. This is certainly possible, and it has been suggested more than once that long-distance alliances and a demand for 'exotica' in distant parts of the country drove production in the fells.[4] However, the situation was far from clear-cut. Other ways of working persisted throughout the life of the outcrop and demand was far from direct. What mattered elsewhere was not simply the remoteness of the source, but the history of the hands through which particular blades had passed and this was also important within the region. The pattern of extraction along the hornstone band owed as much to currents and relations within Cumbria as anywhere else.

We cannot trace the journeys that every blade made, nor the particular reasons for their circulation. To do so would be like trying to keep track of a thousand different rounds of Chinese whispers. What we can identify are some

Skelmore heads. Photo: Helen Evans

of the times and places where those journeys involved the taking of a different path. Beyond the source, the passage of the Neolithic saw the creation of a number of monuments where more extensive geographies became condensed. Some of these sites were on early inventories and itineraries. Recorded by Hutchinson and West from the mid-eighteenth century onwards, a number of Neolithic monuments across the region were recognised as antiquities and incorporated by visitors into their sense of the Picturesque. Incorporation was selective. It was generally those sites with a significant stone component, rather than earthworks, which attracted the attention of most visitors. Places in which the imagination might trace a sense of ruined architectures.[5] Druidical circles and fragmented temples that lent a sense of romantic antiquity and deep-rootedness to the scene, something to balance or anchor the picture. While barrows and other monuments were being recorded by those with more considered antiquarian interests, stone circles held the tourist gaze, an interest that continued throughout the nineteenth century and down to today. Some, like Castlerigg, were even embellished, by decorative fencing or with ornamental plantations of trees to enhance their appearance.

Like tombs, there has been only limited investigation of larger enclosures in Cumbria and it is only recently that some of the earliest of these sites have been recognised. Some bear a strong resemblance to monuments in other regions, and their presence, like non-local flint, is a hint of more extensive networks of contact and communication. One of the more striking of these, at least from the air, is a large enclosure close to Long Meg and her Daughters, a stone circle set within a low bank.[6] The enclosure is at least twice as large as the circle, and the details of its setting suggest that it was already in existence when the stones were set in place. Some appear to stand or lean into the line of the older ditch, and on the side where the two enclosures meet, the arc of the stone circle flattens a little, as if respecting an existing boundary. Another has recently been identified on Aughertree Fell, overlooking the Solway Plain, where interrupted banks and ditches can still be traced on the ground.[7] No doubt there are others still to locate, through aerial survey and the closer examination of sites erroneously assigned to later periods.[8] Enclosures such as Skelmore Heads and Howe Robin, or Carrock Fell.

Superficially at least, these monuments look like causewayed enclosures, circuits of interrupted ditches identified elsewhere in Britain, in Ireland, the Isle of Man and on the Continent. Most comprise earthen banks and ditches, though there are some that were realised in stone; circuits enclosing areas of a hectare or more. They date to the first half of the Neolithic and are some of the most enigmatic monuments to be established in these islands. Some saw use for a generation or two, others for several centuries. A few show signs of sustained occupation, though this is usually quite late in the sequence. Many more contain evidence for an episodic pattern of use, sites more or less abandoned between times when large companies assembled. Places that drew

Mayburgh and King Arthur's Round Table. Crown Copyright: National Monuments Record

a broader world in close before people and herds scattered again along different paths.

Why did people gather in this way? What went on within the line that they drew in earth and stone? Once again, there is a variety in the pattern of events. Evidence from some suggests feasting and other forms of conspicuous consumption, food given or shared when people came together. Some enclosures also witnessed complex rites of passage, the exposure and defleshing of the dead and the destruction or burial of objects that had been associated with people in life. Sometimes this included axes from Cumbria as well as other sources. It would be hard to underestimate the drama of these events. For those who spent a good deal of their time in close company, the scale of a gathering broke with much of experience. A broader world realised as people camped nearby and laboured together in the building or maintenance of the enclosure itself. Crossing the threshold meant entering a special arena; leaving the world of the everyday behind, at least for a time. Here it was possible to contain and attend to important and even dangerous forces. To deal directly with the dead

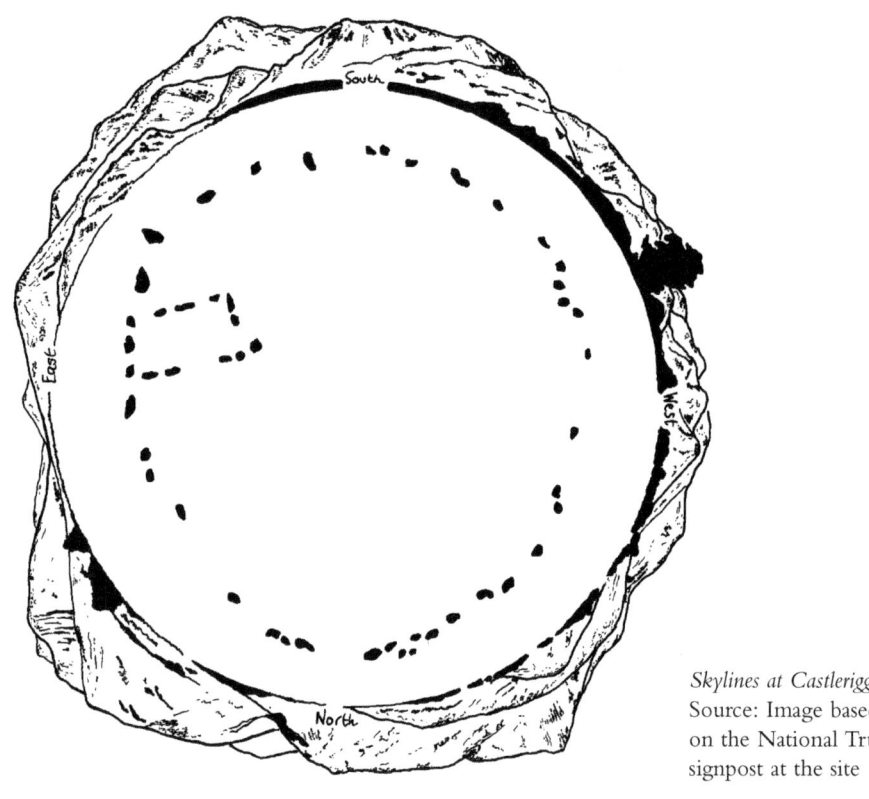

Skylines at Castlerigg.
Source: Image based on the National Trust signpost at the site

and with the spirits of the ancestral past. To deal with others only seen from time to time, to settle disputes and renew alliances. Perspectives were different at these times.

It is no coincidence that these monuments appeared when stock and crops were becoming more widespread. The wild still mattered in many ways, respected and harvested, just as it had always been. But cattle and corn encouraged changes in perception and in the nature of relationships. Tensions over access to land and other resources, concern with fertility and with the debt that was owed to earlier generations. What many enclosures offered was a time and place in which relations between scattered lines could be brought to the fore and dealt with. The dead could also be called upon for help, or to witness important proceedings. Things were different within their bounds and in these charged conditions the broader political contours of the time could be renewed or even redrawn. Threads that ran across the water and into more distant dales. Only further work will demonstrate just how closely the use of enclosures in Cumbria conformed to these patterns. There was no single blueprint and things may have varied, just as later non-conformist chapels in the region departed from the conventions of the established church. But the scale of these places is such that we can envisage broad companies and a confusion of relationships. At least one of the outcomes of these events was the circulation of blades, and it was probably from these points of departure that some began journeys that would take them from hand to hand and out of the region. Across Cumbria and through the Pennines; round the Solway Firth and north; over the water to Ireland.

The local eddies and broader currents that turned around enclosures surfaced again in the later part of the Neolithic. As the third millennium unfolded, a sense of a wider world was realised in the construction of large stone circles and henge monuments. Varied in character, they are found in several parts of the region; in the Eden Valley, to the south and nearer to the western coast. Circles at Castlerigg and Grey Croft and Swinside; the henges of Mayburgh and King Arthur's Round Table. They also have parallels in other parts of Britain and in Ireland, and the larger stone circles may be some of the oldest in Britain.[9]

> . . . *The nature of the ceremonies we do not know; but we can hardly doubt that they included those sacred dances which play a great part in the social life of savages. That these dances were connected with seasonal festivals is, again, likely enough; whenever these circles were erected, their makers were people who tilled the ground and had to watch the turns of the year. How far the circles were designed to help in this, by observing such things as the midsummer sunrise, is a very doubtful matter, and one on which it would be wiser here to say nothing . . .*[10]

Collingwood again, and from the same address; the language a flavour of the academic mentality of his time. A desire to animate the monuments, but a caution over speculative claims of astronomical or calendrical alignments, claims more readily accepted for some circles today. There are hints too of older traditions of enquiry, the use of basic analogy and reference to the crude evolutionary schemes of the later nineteenth century. Though a good deal may have changed since Collingwood's time, his most basic observation about henges and stone circles still holds true; there is much that we do not know. These sites have chequered histories. Some circles have been destroyed; a few because they were feared, many because they were a handy source of millstone or walling. Others had stones removed to allow access to the plough, creating the corduroy ridge and furrow surfaces that can still be seen at places like Long Meg, where Wordsworth sought the utterance of the 'Giant Mother'. Some have even been rebuilt, or used in other ways from the Bronze Age onwards, histories forgotten or reworked in step with broader shifts of attitude. What many suggest is that in Cumbria, as in several other regions, the Later Neolithic was a time when the broader world held a particular importance, when local relations and personal renown were caught up in more extensive networks of contact and alliance.

The settings of these sites are revealing. Some lie on the fringes of the central massif and are set on likely routes of movement around and beyond the region. At Castlerigg, a circle stands on a ridge where several valleys meet, and there are stories that a second circle once stood nearby. The profiles of the stones mimic the surrounding topography, as if to draw a broader world in close, and the site is well placed for approaches from several directions. The final climb that reveals the circle also provides the elevation from which to look out towards several major routes; back into the fells and out towards the lower ground. Here and elsewhere, there is a strong association with passes through high ground, with places where routes and rivers come together. Physical confluences that lent themselves to the convergence of people. Rivers were lines of communication, with other areas and perhaps with other worlds. They featured in origin myths and local cosmologies and this contributed some significance to the building of a monument where currents combined. This appears to have been the case at several circles, among them Kemp Howe and Elva Plain, which lies close to the Derwent on a route that leads out of the fells to the lower ground in the north-west. There is a similar trend nearer to the coast, though not so marked. Swinside is set on a rise near where the Duddon runs out from the higher country; Grey Croft is still closer to the sea, with all the potentials for connection that the water allowed. There may well have been more on the low ground, the bite of agriculture, development and religious intolerance leaving nothing but a faint signature in the soil.

Some sites were set in places that were already of historic importance. The stone circle of Long Meg and her Daughters lies close to the older enclosure

Overlapping Worlds

mentioned above. Antiquarian accounts also refer to another circle in an adjacent field which has now been destroyed. Here there was most likely a tradition of gathering and ceremonial that made this an appropriate place to draw the line again. The rise is also well placed for access to the Tyne Gap through the Pennines and to Scotland, and this may have been important from the outset. This happened in other places too; at Shap where circles and avenues were constructed in close proximity, at Castlerigg, Lacra, and in other settings where only a single monument can now be seen. It also happened near Eamont Bridge, where three henges were thrown up, perhaps in short succession. Only two of these survive as prominent features and the surface appearance of King Arthur's Round Table owes at least something to its remodelling as a visitor attraction and tea garden in the late eighteenth century. The third, the Little Round Table, is now no more than a slight bank in an adjacent field. How far tradition was respected when people built anew is something that we do not know. The new monuments may have been both a break with and a nod to the old, just as early churches implied deep roots by imposition on prehistoric sites that were prominent in local imaginations.[11] Perhaps old enclosures acquired negative associations, a change of fortune requiring that a new line be drawn. Perhaps proceedings required movement between enclosures. Without further investigation in the field, we simply do not know. What

Kemp Howe

Swinside

these accumulations do suggest is the existence of traditions of gathering, an idea of assembly in particular places that was maintained across generations.

> *. . . You can't count them you know. You always get a different number . . .*

These places drew broad companies together, a sense of community realised though labour as well as more formal events. The individual stones at some circles are massive erratics, often granite. They weigh several tons or more and up to a hundred or so people strained together to drag some into place. Many hands on the same line. Long Meg herself, a tall column of red sandstone which stands outside the circle, was probably dragged for more than a mile uphill from beds near the River Eden. The spirals that can be seen on her side may have been carved before the stone made the journey, bringing the associations of a place of ritual communication into a close relationship with the circle. Carvings have also been identified at Little Meg nearby, and at circles such as Castlerigg and Shap. Like others in the region, these designs are similar to those found on passage graves in Ireland.

The banks and ditches of the henge known as King Arthur's Round Table made similar demands on labour at a dramatic scale. Hacking into ditches with

Tokens at Long Meg

antler, stone and timber, heaping up the banks with shoulder blades and baskets. The gentle curves of the banks and ditches we see today, usually on our own, bear only a superficial relation to the original features and the press of numbers as work on the project unfolded. Mayburgh, a few hundred metres to the west, is even more dramatic. In this case, the site was built by the piling up of millions of river cobbles to create huge banks that still stand to a height of several metres. You can see them poking through the uneven turf and in exposures where the clenched roots of trees have lost their hold on the bank. Approached from the east, the impressive façade and entrance to the site is given added prominence by its position on an old river terrace. It is ironic that the reconciliation of management and land use has now drawn a fence line across this approach.

A sense of the river runs through the place; terraces a foundation and water-worn stone a part of its fabric. There were also several large standing stones in the interior and at the entrance, though all but one of these have been removed.[12] Here again, the act of building the monument was a signal event, one that involved a company at odds with much of day-to-day experience. When the time was right, these places were alive with people, a profusion of camps and animals. The young gathering windfalls for the fires, the renewal of acquaintances and the appraisal of other herds. Labour at a scale that had few parallels; kin and relative strangers in close proximity. Chains of people linked together in ways that were not possible at other times.

As with older enclosures, it makes little sense to assume that circles and henges were founded for a single purpose. And to say, as some have done, that they were established primarily to coordinate the trade of axes is to put the cart before the horse. An association with axes can certainly be made. Blades were recovered from Mayburgh and Grey Croft, and from Castlerigg, where a miniature axe was also recently found. These demonstrate an association, deposits linked to funerary rites or buried as offerings for some other purpose. Roughouts and polished blades, even some half-finished forms, have been found relatively close as well; at Clifton, near Mayburgh, Kell Bank, near Grey Croft and at Hunsonby, not far from Long Meg. These certainly suggest a connection with the people who gathered at certain times. But blades were just an element in the flow of things. There were many axes to grind when people came together.

The circle was both inclusive and exclusive. A threshold and a boundary, it could be drawn upon in different ways. Where the banks of a henge rose around proceedings, there was a sense of important rites and forces contained by the perimeter. Only some could cross at certain times, while others

Lacra

Long Meg Monolith. Copyright Beckensall, 2002

remained outside. There was secrecy as spirits were called upon and initiates instructed; words that could not be spoken beyond the bounds. Things were laid bare in the arena. Distances collapsed: between people, and perhaps between the living and the dead. Proceedings could be highly charged, people mindful of the consequences if the right respect was not shown or if their performance did not go well. Being allowed to enter, to officiate or to have knowledge of the forces harnessed at these times was a prerogative of varied companies. Those with a certain standing; those who had reached the appropriate age; those with the right connections. These were powerful concerns and they bled into other aspects of life. What happened at these places had implications long after people had scattered.

These were fluid and inclusive times, some inside, others stood on banks or higher ground to follow events; processions, dances and other tournaments of value. And always, a mess of people attending to other things. This would have been easy at King Arthur's Round Table, where the terrace of an ancient river rises up to mimic one side of the monument, the line marked now by a tired hedgeline and numerous rabbit burrows. Here it is also possible that proceedings involved processions between monuments. As some sat and talked around their fires, others moved from the public arena of King Arthur's Round Table to the great enclosure of Mayburgh, where events inside were more easily hidden from the gaze of those outside. At circles too, the positions of stones lent themselves to the ordering of events. Thresholds to be crossed between portal stones, oratory to attend to as people sat or stood with their backs to the granite. A celebration, invocation, or meeting between the heads of different lines may have been accompanied by feasts and by dancing, the rhythms of the moment echoed by the stones themselves. Lit by fires at night, they too may have joined the dance.

These moments, in their turn, took place against a powerful backdrop. Gatherings were seasonal and sometimes synchronised with cycles in the sky. Astronomical alignments have been claimed for a number of circles, particularly those with outliers, or with one stone made of a different material. Though these lack the mathematical precision sought by some, a relationship with cardinal and solar alignments is certainly there, at places like Swinside and Long Meg, at Castlerigg and Brats Hill. In a world where the fertility of the land, of stock and kin were powerful concerns, these connections should not surprise us. When life was bound to a seasonal wheel, where cycles were recognised in the land and in the lives of people, these links with thresholds in the year meant many things. A signal for planting, or a start to a ceremony in the season of the dead, an anticipated time when the land would be born again if all went well. Where the sun participated in the gathering, the order of the present was tied to tradition, and tradition in turn to the timeless. The stones themselves were implicated in the process, reinforcing statements through the simple fact of their endurance.

A mess of exchanges were woven through these proceedings. The to and fro of trade as people camped around a clearing; stock, blades and other things moving between different families. There were also more directed and politically charged transactions; bouts of giving conducted in front of an audience. Gifts of food and of tokens such as blades which passed from one line to another, counter-gifts to balance long-standing obligations. Links were made between these transactions and those more timeless cycles that were cut into the sky. And because some debts could only be discharged in special circumstances, the periodic use of these monuments gave gifts a sense of duration. When people scattered at the close, these tokens travelled with them. With them also went initiates, new stock and perhaps new kin; news and ideas to circulate around home fires. On the coast, on shelves above the Eden Valley, and even further afield. Amongst other things, the blades they carried would remind them of the ties that bound them to others. Relations remembered as an axe was turned to a task; authorities recalled when another was taken from the rafters to be displayed or handed on in another round. There would be much to talk about until the next gathering. For some blades, the journey had just begun.

> . . . *My father said he turned it up with the plough. It was in the drawer for years until we had a clear out after he died. I'd forgotten all about it. He'd sometimes fish it out and tell us that's how much things had changed since his day! I think we even believed him . . .*

CHAPTER 9

ENDINGS

. . . I hate the Countryside so much . . .[1]

There is an anecdote that hangs around many slate quarries. You hear it in Wales and in Cumbria and no doubt elsewhere. The owner was showing a guest around the site, a man of some importance and considerable wealth; a potential investor. As they came close to the face, the visitor gestured up to a precarious ledge where an older man was sitting motionless upon the slate. Taken aback by the lack of effort and counting the cost even then, he shouted up to ask what the old man was doing. 'Thinking' was his reply.

The story has an obvious meaning. It draws a line of understanding between those who do the work and those who reap the financial rewards. It highlights a skill in reading stone. Without close inspection and introspection, charges could be badly set; blows could be struck against the run of the slate. Valuable stone could be lost and the chance of death or injury increased. You might assess the relative importance of these outcomes differently depending on where you are in the story. What it also reveals is different a sense of looking close altogether sharper than the focus of the Romantic gaze. A perspective that saw stone and potential, biography and social history all at once. An eye that took time to develop. The old man on the slate provides no immediate parallel for the people who worked around the Langdales five thousand years ago. But he does remind us that beyond the grander and detached perspectives, there are always ways of seeing and of working that merge biography with history. If the path this book has taken has led us anywhere, it is hopefully to

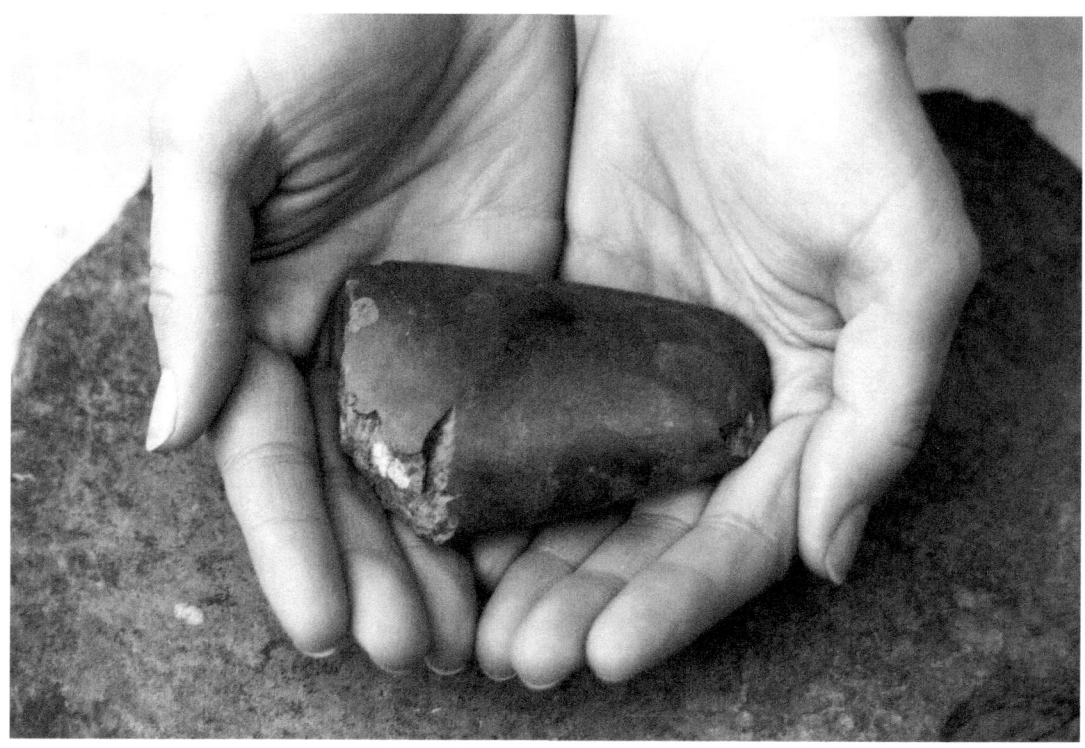

Burnt and broken Cumbrian axe recovered from Haddenham, Cambs

the view that things were no less complex in the Neolithic, only different.

The quarry where I first heard about the old man is long since closed, the story itself part of the more recent romance that is building up around the place. Quarrying ceased in the 1960s and some who might have once expected to work there now travel to Sellafield. One of the few things of which we can be certain is that the end of quarrying at Langdale did not come at such a price. Just when this happened is unclear, in part because the process unfolded over generations. Work did not simply stop overnight, some equivalent for the downing of tools or the locking of gates. Abandonment was gradual, a slow falling away from the stone in the grey area that blurs the Neolithic into the Early Bronze Age. We catch only glimpses of this process. We know from pollen and from chance finds that the Langdales continued to be a focus for grazing throughout the second millennium BC and beyond. A Bronze Age presence is suggested by scatters of cairns in Mickleden and by the low banks and small circular structures on the higher ground on the north side of the valley. At the moment, these do no more than hint that occupation in the area came to be more sustained over the period. This trend can be traced across much of the central fells and it tells us that as the third millennium gave way to the second, the Langdales probably came 'closer to home'. The required journey lost some of its distance and its significance.

Perception of the stone also seems to have shifted. Axe blades are known from Early Bronze Age contexts, but the numbers are small and there is little to indicate sustained working at the source or elsewhere. Across the region, there are also scatters which contain a few simple tools of the same volcanic tuff, including a small number of barbed and tanged arrowheads which were being made across the transition we have constructed between the two periods. Most could easily be the result of reworking older blades and there are many which show signs of being worked down to some degree, even simple flake tools with elements of older polish still visible on their surface. This probably happened throughout the sequence, the stone finding uses long after a cutting edge was lost. But in time, older tools and stream worn pebbles became the only sources people recognised through use. There are also a few perforated implements such as maceheads which probably date to the same late phase. These may have been made at the source, but there is little to suggest that working was anything other than ad hoc; evidence for these later implements is very thin on the ground indeed. It is probably unwise to assume that no axe blades at all were made in the earliest phases of the Bronze Age; some probably were. But this bore little relation to the traditions of working seen on the crags in earlier generations.

From the nineteenth century onwards, the erosion of these traditions has often been explained as a result of the introduction of bronze. Driven by the clattering momentum of industrial innovation, many scholars at the time cast bronze artefacts as inherently superior, seeing this as the reason why axes were no longer made at specific stone sources. Like the Three Age system itself, such arguments are so familiar that we treat them now as common sense. The trouble is that they don't really work. The earliest bronze axes and daggers could certainly be used and often were. But they were by no means all that strong or necessarily that much better than their counterparts in traditional materials. Some of the first metal items were also what we would class as bodily adornments. Not only that, flint and other stone remained important in the making of many tools. These were often fairly simple, but there are arrowheads, daggers and perforated implements which reflect a considerable, even greater, investment of time and skill than that given to earlier axes. Some of these turn up in burials and other formal deposits during the early stages of the Bronze Age, present as tokens of identity and value. Stone and skill in its working still mattered then. It was simply that concern no longer extended to the hornstone or to the making of distinctive grey-green blades.

This shift of perception was encouraged by qualities in metal that went beyond utility. Ores were not found everywhere and the knowledge required in working them was complex. Extraction, processing and the casting of metal were also dangerous tasks. Transforming striking minerals; the poisons, danger and drama of smelting. These qualities have often encouraged the view that working is a potent or magical act, one to be shrouded in complex proscriptions. Metalworkers in different settings can be a separate caste, polluting and threatening, or of elevated stature. Alchemists, magicians or the lowest of the low. Sometimes they are just like everyone else; changing only for a while when they turn to ore and hearth. Metal could also be decorated or embellished and moulds modified. It could be recycled and manipulated in ways which had no strong counterpart in stone. An axe or a dagger could be turned back into liquid and rendered into new and varied forms. Traded goods could be turned into appropriate gifts and refashioned in keeping with local convention. Beyond everything else, metal had a potential to catch the light and perhaps to hold the imagination, even the distinctive colours of the ores invited interpretation.

These qualities made bronze a more than appropriate material for the making of tokens of identity and value. It was this, rather than any significant functional advantage, which changed the ways that stone blades were regarded. New forms took their place on the shoulder, changing hands when people came together, some acquiring names and biographies as they moved. The messages may have gone largely unchanged; it was the medium that was different. Once this happened, perception of the hornstone and of the crags began to change. It no longer mattered to use the stone in customary ways, to maintain traditional journeys to the source or to raise familiar hammers and address named crags. The stone still had its uses, but it was no longer what it was. In time, even the act of working itself lost much of its shape; learning no longer so important for what it said about you.

How far metal ores were extracted in Cumbria, if at all, is impossible to say. The later and extensive history of mining in the area demonstrates the potential, but it has also worked over so much ground that we cannot yet tell if this was realised. All we have to go on is the occasional recovery of distinctive stone hammers around areas like Coniston. It may be significant though that at the Great Orme on the North Wales coast, somewhere visible from the fells on a very clear day, copper was being extracted in the Early Bronze Age. The Orme is little more than a stone's throw from Craig Lwyd, the long used source of Group VII axes. Here perhaps, the history of working in the area encouraged communities to recognise the new potential and incorporate it into local traditions. That might have also happened in Cumbria; work on new materials coming to play some of the roles that journeys to the hornstone had once fulfilled. However, in a world that was lived for the most part at local and regional scales, things may have taken a different path, only time and further work will tell.

For fifteen hundred years or so, the crags around the Langdales were one of the most prominent communal monuments in the region. Work was hard and dangerous. It involved skills that took time to polish and a knowledge of the stone that was practical, social and entirely of its time. But times

Endings

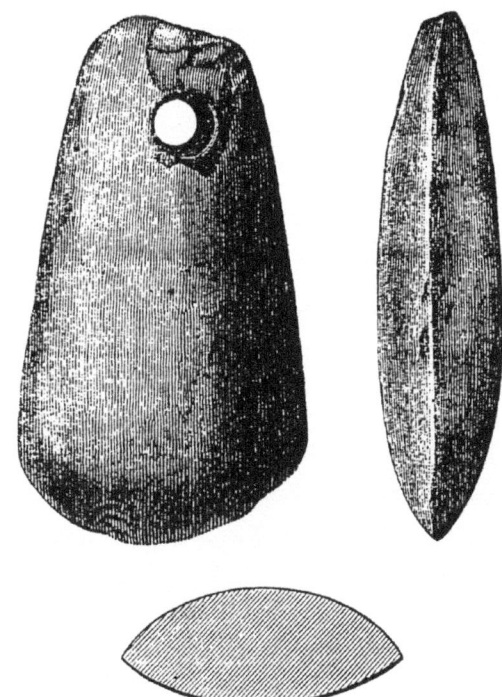

Worn and reworked axe blade perforated for suspension

changed and people found new ways of presenting themselves and dealing with others. Slowly, perhaps imperceptibly, the stone began to settle. Vegetation encroached upon the edges of scree, lichen on the scars of old faces. Echoes faded. For many, the distinctive profile on the skyline became somewhere that was gestured to most often in stories of the past or in discussions of stock.

Axes had their endings too. Over much of the Neolithic, many were simply worked to exhaustion and lost or discarded in ways that prompted little comment. They slipped quietly from view, diminished from years of use or thrown to one side when a well-worn edge finally broke beyond repair. Others were handed on or down, a routine reminder of the line that ran between people. Some small blades were even drilled to hang upon a belt, on a necklace, perhaps in the gear of a grandchild or the paraphernalia of a ritual specialist. There are not many of these, but the fact that there are any demonstrates that even when it could no longer be used, a blade could sometimes still be valued, was still worth holding onto.

The stories in others were important enough to require close attention when things changed. When a person died or a relationship ended, it was sometimes necessary to mark that shift by treating a blade in a particular way. As bodies began the process of decay that marked a different sort of journey, tools carried in life were encouraged to travel with them. Smashed or thrown into rivers during rites of passage, even burnt to release the spirit from the stone. This happened in many areas. At the enclosures of Haddenham and Etton in the Fens, Cumbrian blades that had seen years of use were buried with some formality without their cutting edges. Some were also burnt, smooth planes shattered into blocky and irregular terrain by angular fractures in the fire. At these places where scattered communities sometimes gathered, the breaking of the body of the blade ran parallel to the treatment accorded to peoples' remains. Other blades were released as offerings or as burial tokens, in rivers, caves and at other monuments. In each case, what mattered was biography.

This also happened in Cumbria, another sign that value was locally understood, not just a product of distance. Blades recovered from monuments, from wet ground and from fissures; chance losses, offerings and accompaniments to ashes. On Sizergh Fell, where the Langdales are a distinctive profile on the distant north-east horizon, a blade was buried in a gryke on a natural limestone knoll. Even close by, there is little to distinguish the knoll from two burial mounds raised on the fell around the end of the Neolithic. Perhaps the distinction did not matter at the time. Near to the blade were a couple of flakes from another and a polissoir, its grinding surface dished and smooth. The axe showed signs of having been burnt and had split in the fire.

Cumbrian axe buried in a pit at Etton, Cambridgeshire. Photo: Francis Pryor

These tokens could have been laid to rest in this low knoll for any number of reasons. Like deposits found elsewhere in the region, the arrangement suggests a considered act focused on distinctive natural features. Places which were significant as mythic mounds, as ancestral remains or the traces of past events. Did it happen alongside the interment of ashes nearby, the burnt blade taken from the pyre for a burial of its own? Was some other spirit or connection with the place invoked by the offering? We will never know. All we can say is that eventually all axe blades left the hand; lying hidden until the time came to be turned into thunderbolts and collectables.

The path does not of course end there; it just becomes more difficult to follow for a time. We do not know when old blades were first recognised as thunderbolts, or given restorative powers. A few years or centuries, a millennium or more – who knows? We don't know the stories told by Roman soldiers garrisoned at Hardknot nor the names, if any, given to the crags by Anglian or Norse shepherds. It may be that an older name for the Pike of Stickle – Steel Pike – reflects an awareness of roughouts on the fells, even if these were mistaken for hones or sharpening stones. Some say that 'Strickle' was the old Norse for a whetstone, but it may just as easily have been the shape of the mountain which invited the name.

There doesn't have to be a single answer; there seldom is. Even now, the same grey-green blades circulate for all sorts of reasons, the forms of our attention the product of who we are. An heirloom on the mantelpiece, an artefact anatomised upon the page, a fact in the darkness of an archive, the odd stone amongst cobbles, the keepsake in the kitchen drawer, a price in the auction room, a sharp tooth bedded in the fabric of a wall. It's the same for the crags themselves, which have taken nigh on four thousand years to emerge again as a monument of sorts. A home, a living, a place to find renewal in company or alone, an Area of Outstanding Natural Beauty (AONB), a sort of national property, a place in which some feel more welcome than others. For my own part, the writing of this book has brought home just how difficult it is to reconcile these different perceptions and the scales at which they operate. The crags certainly impose themselves upon the senses, but responses to their presence have been, and remain, a function of history and identity.

The journey has also made me realise that the practice of landscape archaeology itself owes far more to the Romantic tradition than I was initially prepared to accept. The image of the solitary figure walking and gazing upon the land is a persistent one, present in recent experiments which have tried to infer the past meanings of monuments through the bodily experience of their spaces. Those experiences are, I think, essential. Walking, scrambling and even working the stone have, for me, been central to thinking about the material experience of people on the crags over four or five thousand years ago. A form of 'looking close', they have inevitably shaped the interpretative process. I make no apologies for the fact that they have also been a pleasure, that I have been privileged to call them 'work'. Unlike Wordsworth, however, I cannot say that I have taken the same path as the sower, the shepherd or stoneworker. I have come to the place from a very different world and the very fact that much of my time has been spent on my own has itself set a limit. Only when I worked on the fells as part of an excavation team did I begin to recognise that the company one keeps is just as important. That is what we miss when we tread, often without thinking, in the steps of the Solitary, the Wanderer and the Poet. And if we miss that, then we lose sight of the communities that were once created by the work; the path simply takes us back to ourselves.

The legacy of the Romantic tradition also works through landscape archaeology in another way. Where discussion turns around small settlements or concepts of kinship and affiliation, there is a danger that we perpetuate a tinted and insular view. A world in which boundaries were close, relations small scale, stable and harmonious. At best, the image is easily recruited to foster a sentimental nostalgia for a past that never really existed. At worst, it lends itself to pernicious myths of Englishness which have no place in either present or past. If the spread of axe blades tells us anything at all, it is that boundaries don't really work like that. We are always a part of many communities and what matters is how we connect or overlap with one another. How that was possible then and how we deal with it now, those are the questions.

A LONG LABOUR

He'd spotted the roughout the second time he'd scrambled out of the valley. Under Gimmer, up through Middle Gully then across towards an unbroken view of the Pike. Still getting his eye in, he'd stopped to rest against a narrow ledge where hooves had scoured the bilberry and exposed the old scree. Lying in a nest of flakes, it looked perfect – the grey-blue stone faceted by the scars of confident working. An egg that had never hatched.

It was only when he'd picked it up, turned it in his hand, that he'd seen the problem. A large lump, bulbous and irregular. A buttress jutting out from the more gradual slope, sides stepped and fractured by repeated hammering. Someone had tried and failed to bring symmetry to the stone. He thought about the muttered curse, the letting go and the move on to another blank. What names were taken in vain, where was the stubborn stone consigned to in the imagination of the maker? Did it matter, or was this part of the transaction with the place? It had been too long.

After that it became a habit, a little ritual. However he left the valley, all routes ended there. Each time he climbed, he found himself below the ledge, checking that it hadn't strayed, turning it in his hand, pushing the lump with his thumb. And each time he descended, the roughout went with him, turning in his mind's eye, the focus always on the flaw. Scales merged, the contours and profile of the piece indivisible from the crags. *It could be done.* It was a question of getting the angle right; letting the hammer fall where the buttress met the slope. Hands went through the motions, reducing the imagined stone. Could it be worked after such an interval? Had frost crept in, forcing cracks to divert the strike? Was it a conceit to even try? For a handful of years, and as many scrambles, the roughout was raised and balanced, only to be returned to rest below the ledge.

Three years later, he found himself at the top of the crag, a beach stone in the bag on his shoulder. He browsed on bilberries, letting the fruit burst between his teeth as he traversed to find the ledge once more. It was still there, pressed down and partly buried in the scree, lanolin on the ridges a vestige of sheep sheltering from the wind. Raised again, it sat easily in the hand, fingers resting in the facets as he exhaled his indecision in the smoke of a final cigarette. *Best get to it.*

A tap from the cobble told him that the stone was still true. Any mistake would be of his making and not the fault of the frost. He held the roughout against his thigh, the lump pressed into his flesh, and made a few slow practise strokes. The focus came down, balanced on the blade's edge. A breath later he struck, the hammer falling close to the line, the impact absorbed by his body. There was a dull crack, the sound of stone parting company with stone and he pulled the roughout away. The lump remained behind, pressed to his thigh for a moment before slipping down to clatter amongst the flakes below. He leant forward and picked it up, placed it back into the concavity made by its departure. A perfect fit; none closer. The contours now were smooth and regular, the new scar a fresh blue-green against a weathered background. *Lucky devil.* The knot unravelling between his shoulders, he let the flake fall back into the nest and descended with the roughout in the bag.

Away from the source, the way was easier; glacial rather than seismic. Hours bearing down on a slab of grit, a straight line between shoulder and stone. Ridges reduced to lower ground, the hollows of each scar softened and erased. Checking the line by hand and eye, curving the cutting edge and levelling the facets on each side. As many hours again with water and fine silt, puckered fingers ingrained with a tracery of grey. Three days to bring out the colour and the lustre. After that, it was done. A finish felt as much as seen. Roughout to axe blade in five thousand years.

NOTES
BIBLIOGRAPHY
INDEX

NOTES

CHAPTER 1

1. The Picturesque was a successor to earlier traditions of landscape portraiture. In a highly persuasive account, Dennis Cosgrove argues that the depiction of landscape as an object within a frame emerged hand in hand with an economy that viewed land as a commodity to be bought and sold (Cosgrove 1984; see also Berger 1973; Barrell 1980). The link with capitalism is well made, but there were other currents too, among them a tendency for many European states to draw upon representations of the land to characterise a sense of national identity.
2. Claude glasses were hand-held viewing frames that allowed people to compose picturesque scenes, screening out the extraneous and the unsightly. Many contained convex mirrors to create panoramic views, or were designed to take inserts of tinted glass so that the scene could be given the colour of different seasons or times of day. This was taken to its logical conclusion at Claife, the first of Thomas West's 'stations' for the viewing of Windermere. Built in 1799 at the behest of the Revd William Braithwaite, it was extended soon after by the Curwens of Belle Isle. Together with the temple at Storrs and Belle Isle itself, Claife Station formed a scene full of classical reference for those with the eyes to see it. It also had tinted windows.
3. At a time of war with France, when national identity was a major political concern, the creation of 'classic ground' within the boundaries of Britain, even of England, was powerful propaganda (Newman 1987; Williams 1973). In the end, it went even further than that, becoming a feature of the consolidation of Empire. The names we associate with the Lake District can be found in many countries, and Wendy Darby suggests that one of the features of the colonial experience in places like Australia and Tasmania was the recreation of the picturesque outing amongst scenery deemed equivalent to that found amongst the Lakes (Darby 2000).

4. This soon changed. By the nineteenth century, there was a backlash against grand and sometimes classically inspired buildings. These bore little resemblance to the vernacular architectures of the region and unlike many traditional buildings, they often stood out (to get the best views). When John Ruskin came to live by Coniston at Brantwood in the 1870s, he made much of the fact that his buildings were in keeping with the 'cottage' architectures of the region.

5. Apparently, it was not just the echoes. The cannon heightened hearing so that when silence fell, you gained a sharper sense of hearing sufficient to catch more distant waterfalls. What many were really were listening for was a report of themselves (Nicholson 1959). Such views invited caricature, nowhere more sharply captured than in *The tour of Dr Syntax in search of the Picturesque*, a thinly veiled dig at Gilpin. Published in 1812, and illustrated to great effect by Thomas Rowlandson, it enjoyed a wide popularity and spawned many imitations. It includes the doctor's response to a weathered waymarker encountered on a moor:

> *I'll make a drawing of the post;*
> *And tho' a flimsy taste may flout it,*
> *There's something picturesque about it;*
> *'Tis rude and rough, without a gloss,*
> *And is well cover'd o'er with moss;*
> *And I've a right – (who dares deny it?)*
> *To place yon group of asses by it.*
> *Aye! this will do: and now I'm thinking,*
> *That self same pond where Grizzle's drinking,*
> *If hither brought t'would better seem,*
> *And faith I'll turn it to a stream:*
> *I'll make this flat a shaggy ridge,*
> *And o'er the water throw a bridge:*
> *I'll do as other sketchers do –*
> *Put anything into the view;*
> *And any object recollect,*
> *to add a grace and give effect.*
> *Thus, though from truth I haply err,*
> *The scene preserves its character.*
> *What man of taste my right can doubt,*
> *To put things in or leave them out?*
> *Tis more than right, it is a duty,*
> *If we consider landscape beauty:*
> *He ne'er will as an artist shine*
> *Who copies Nature line by line:*
> *Whoe'er from nature takes a view,*
> *Must copy and improve it too.*
> *To heighten ev'ry work of art,*
> *Fancy should take an active part:*
> *Thus I (which few I think can boast)*
> *Have made a landscape of a post.*

6. These issues continue to turn in political debate and in artistic responses. Only a few years ago, an installation at Grizedale Sculpture Park provoked heated exchanges. The cause of the argument was a series of brown 'heritage' style signs which, with tongue in cheek and a definite point to make, directed walkers to 'good views'. Another installation inserted the logos of outdoor clothing into mundane landscape features, highlighting the fetishistic attraction that we are encouraged to have for a superfluity of gear.

7. In the latter decades of the eighteenth century, twice as many people lived in the country as in the city or in towns. Forty years later, that equation had been reversed. This fed a sentimental nostalgia for, and re-evaluation of, the countryside (Williams 1973). It also created a larger and more varied audience for the image.

8. Higham 1986; Phythian-Adams 1991.

9. Collingwood 1932. Collingwood's arguments are certainly of their time, as are his solutions to problems of interpretation (eg. Collingwood 1946). That said, his contention that the study of the past is, in part at least, an imaginative and creative act, is as important now as it was then, perhaps even more so.

10. Pennington 1970, 1975; Tipping 1994; Tooley 1981; Walker 1966.
11. Bradley & Edmonds 1993; Fell 1988.
12. Burl 1976. Precisely how many circles were constructed in the Neolithic, and how many belong to the earlier part of the Bronze Age, remains the subject of much argument. The problem is at its most acute with the smaller examples and is not helped by the fact that our systems of classification tend to vary and to overlap, so that one person sees a small stone circle where another sees a kerbed cairn or a ringcairn.
13. In western Cumbria, sequences often reveal declines in the frequency of elm pollen in the earlier fourth millennium. This has been seen by some as a consequence of clearance and by others as a symptom of disease. Though the jury is still out on this, the elm decline has often been taken as the point where the two periods divide.
14. Thomas 1999.
15. The character, scale and duration of earlier Neolithic settlement are very difficult to tie down. The relative scarcity of buildings in most regions has led some to suggest that people were essentially mobile. Others point out that the buildings that are known may well be the few that have survived and that their presence indicates a largely sedentary existence. The debate is easily and unhelpfully polarised, often missing the fact that things may have been very different from one area to another (Cooney 2000; Darvill & Thomas 1996; Whittle 2003). What we do know is that there are no settlements with definitive evidence for continuous occupation throughout the Neolithic. This suggests that in some regions, there were cycles of movement resolved at scales of time measured across generations. In the shorter term, movement may well have been a routine part of life. But this often took the form of what Alasdair Whittle has called 'tethered mobility', the periodic or seasonal movement of some (and occasionally all) of a community between different settings (Whittle 1998; Pollard 1999). Though longer and more specialised journeys were made from time to time, the distances routinely travelled in many areas were often measured in handfuls of days.
16. Bradley 1998, 2000; Edmonds 1999; Tilley 1994; Whittle 1996.
17. Barrett 1994.
18. Thomas 1999.
19. This problem of scale is fundamental. Our tendency to pitch syntheses of prehistory at the level of the British Isles often glosses over important regional differences. It is also not uncommon to find one well studied region (usually in the south) being extrapolated out to interpret other regions which actually have a very different balance of evidence. When models work at these grand (or even grander) scales, they automatically miss the scales at which peoples' lives unfolded in the past. Moreover, to talk of Neolithic 'Britain' or more bizarre still 'England' is to project two political fields back beyond their historical roots. That is how origin myths work.
20. In the very different setting of the Pacific, Chris Gosden has pointed out that island communities, separated by far greater distances, maintained regular contact with each other through voyages back and forth. Why should we assume that a stretch of water that you can sometimes see across would have been an impassable barrier?
21. Darbishire 1873.
22. The importance of the water is illustrated in several places in the account when Darbishire talks of wooden artefacts drying out, shrinking or crumbling to nothing.

The Langdales

CHAPTER 2

1. Evans, J. 1897: 58. Evans records a wealth of evidence, from the classical sources onwards, for the view that axes were thunderbolts with remarkable restorative powers. Some were specifics for rheumatism, others promoted sleep or prevented 'rot or putrid decay'. Apparently you could tell they were thunderbolts because of the burnt smell of the stone when freshly broken. Some 'relics' appear to have been circulated within families or communities over several centuries.
2. Bradley 1984.
3. Gosden 1999.
4. '. . . It weighs six and a quarter pounds, and measures seventeen and five eighths inches in length. . .' (Evans 1897: 118). A hallmark of work from an early stage has been the meticulous description of blades as a basis for their classification. Reports frequently detail the shape, length, breadth and weight of blades in a language which would not be out of place in the *Angling Times*. Such work is important, but we should not conclude from this that the only things that mattered about an artefact are things that we can measure.
5. In an excellent discussion of the changing relationship between archaeology and anthropology, Chris Gosden makes the point that the displays in places like the Pitt-Rivers Museum were designed to educate, to put across a particular view of the world, its order and its origins (Gosden 1999). This was certainly persuasive. As late as the 1930s, it was not uncommon to find books about prehistory in which drawings of Old Stone Age hunter-gatherers were based on photographs of Australian Aborigines. By contrast, images of the New Stone Age were populated by Caucasians.
6. Kendrick, T. 1925: 126. Kendrick goes on to suggest that '. . . in this Neolithic awakening of Europe, it may be that the symbol of the advance, the hall-mark of the new culture, was the stone axe . . . it was at once the signal for and the sign of cultural improvement . . . (*ibid.*: 133)
7. Barnes 1963; Bradley & Edmonds 1993; McIntyre, 1937; Pitts 1996. An early commentator on axe blades recovered in Cumbria was Canon Rawnsley, one of the founders of the National Trust.
8. Manby 1979.
9. Knowles 1906.
10. Fell 1964. Much of the story of the stone axe in Cumbria was written by Clare Fell. One of the first to write in detail about the sources and about the distinctive forms of blades from the region, she could recognise almost every one by sight. When I first met her, she was living in Arnside, in the south of the region. Her house gave her a view across the estuary and up through low hills and high fells straight to the Langdales. She said that though she could no longer climb, she could still make the journey with her eyes.
11. Grimes gives a fascinating account of the history and development of implement petrology in Britain. He also notes how the now widespread practice of removing sections or cores from stone axes and other forms had first to overcome the reluctance of archaeologists and owners who regarded the artefacts as sacrosanct (Grimes 1979: 1-4). Many still do; the numbers appearing on distribution maps are a minimum.
12. By 1988, some 1,612 axes had been identified as Group VI. See Clough & Cummins 1979 & 1988 for a description and discussion of this ongoing project.

13. The work continues and has recently been extended by the systematic research of the Irish Stone Axe Project (Cooney & Mandal 1998). This has identified over a hundred Group VI axes. Some of these may have been made on more locally derived and closely similar material, but most are the result of a journey across the water.
14. This argument for a national trade was an inversion of nineteenth-century accounts, which saw a developed sense of trade as a hallmark of more complex or 'evolved' societies than those which scholars of the time assumed they were dealing. This owed more than a little to the simple caricature of trade and exchange systems in societies encountered outside the west. In the twentieth century, discussion of large-scale industries and of a national trading network did not, however, go unchallenged. Graham Clark suggested that modern economic principles were not entirely appropriate to the study of prehistory (Clark 1965; see also Bradley & Edmonds 1993; Phillips 1979).
15. Stephen Briggs has argued for some time that the interpretation of distribution patterns has paid insufficient attention to the contribution of glacial erratics (Briggs 1976; 1989). Echoing the argument about the origins of the bluestones at Stonehenge, Briggs' observations are important. Erratics were certainly used, though the scale of their contribution cannot as yet be assessed. However, in the face of literal mountains of working debris at sources in Cumbria, County Antrim and North Wales, and the persistence of several distinctive forms, it is likely that in many areas, the contribution was relatively small. In any case, the journey to the source was itself important, not just the stone.
16. Darbishire 1873; Evans 1897.
17. Weiner 1985; Thomas 1991.
18. Shee Twohig 1981; Edmonds 1995; Thomas & Tilley 1993.
19. It has been suggested more than once that alongside their occasional interment as grave goods, axes were often deposited and sometimes broken up with some formality in other settings as a feature of rites of passage (Edmonds 1999; Oswald et al. 2000; Pryor 1998; Thomas 1999).
20. An abundance of stone axes, including Cumbrian blades, has long been recognised in the Thames, where extensive dredging has brought in a good catch (Adkins & Jackson 1978). Some are no doubt there as a result of chance losses and erosion. However, Richard Bradley has made a convincing argument that many entered the water as a function of more considered rites; even as acts of gift exchange with gods and local spirits (Bradley 1990).

CHAPTER 3

1. West 1778.
2. William Gilpin's *Observations* (1786) and Uvedale Price's *Essays on the Picturesque* (1794) make extensive reference to the importance of trees in different settings; as objects of attention in their own right and as a part of specific scenes. For Gilpin, trees could be used to frame or balance a view, and if this meant moving or simply adding them to the image, so be it. Price, like Ruskin nearly a century later, talked more specifically about the revelations that could be had in studying form. He was less concerned with grand prospects and pictorialism and argued for a closer focus, seeing in the form and setting of trees the richness of Nature and the process of 'benign neglect' which had shaped the land.

The Langdales

3. One of the earliest and most influential expressions of this was the publication of John Evelyn's *Silva, or a discourse of Forest-Trees* (1664). In an eclectic volume which moves from the practical to the poetic, Eveleyn makes an explicit parallel between the restoration of the monarchy and the re-establishment of England's woodland heritage.
4. Daniels 1988; Schama 1995.
5. Lynn Linton 1864 (*The Lake Country*). For a more extensive discussion of woodlands and their uses, see Rackham 1990.
6. Place names containing the word *Savin* or *Savins*, a reference to juniper, can still be found in areas where the species was persistently harvested for charcoal.
7. Winchester 1987.
8. 'In Norse mythology the gigantic ash Yggdrasil stands as the universal tree with its roots in the nether world and the mythical spring about its base. Its evergreen leaves afford pasture to the stag whose dripping horns watered the earth. Eagles in the highest branches scan the earth, while the tale bearing squirrel *Ratatosk* gossips between the higher and lower denizens of the heavenly and earthly realms . . .' (Davies 1988).
9. Gelling 1984.
10. See Bradley & Edmonds 1993 for a section through part of Langdale Combe.
11. At Blea Tarn, an increase in herbaceous pollen in a pine-birch woodland is recorded at around 3700 BC, a more intensive episode again near the end of the fourth millennium (Pennington 1975; see Bradley & Edmonds 1993 for a more general review of environmental data from the area).
12. Birks 1982; Bonsall *et al.* 1986; Tipping 1994; Pennington 1970; 1975; Walker 1965; 1966; 2001.
13. There has been a long and varied history of surface collection in Cumbria, particularly near the coast, where the work of a few dedicated individuals gives us much of our picture (e.g. Cross 1938; Barnes 1955; 1970; Nickson & Macdonald 1955). To both the west and the east of the fells, the work of the Cherry family from the 1960s onwards has been especially influential (e.g. Cherry & Cherry 1982; 1983; 1987).
14. Brown 1997.
15. Simmons 1995.
16. Harding and Young 1979: 104. I've included this quotation because it is both sufficient and insufficient. It tells you how working with a stone axe is different from working with its counterpart in steel. What it doesn't show you is how that difference is realised in bodily terms.

CHAPTER 4

1. See for example Nicholson 1963.
2. Tyler 1994.
3. Working the wad at Seathwaite was always small scale, employing only a handful of people underground (Boon 1976; Bridge 1992; Tyler 1995). Yet the mineral was so valuable that guard houses were erected to protect the Upper and Lower Wadholes and by the eighteenth century theft became a felony (see also Adams 1988 and Postlethwaite 1913).
4. Tyler 1995.
5. A significant expansion in the scale of quarrying came in the mid-nineteenth century with the development of the railway network and the knock-on effect that this had

on demand for building. This prompted considerable protest from those who sought to protect and conserve the area. From then on, quarrying was regarded by many as an unwelcome intrusion, though not perhaps by those who made a profit or a living from the enterprise.

6. The names of peaks and individual crags can be traced back to different sources and many have more than one. Some have roots in Old Norse, while others relate to specific associations built up during farming or industrial activity over the last few centuries. Some, like Esk Pike, have only recently been named, in this case as a product of the interest of climbers and walkers. The terms of reference change depending on who you are and the nature of your connection.
7. Robinson 1709; Johnson 1988; Marshall & Davies-Shiel 1977.
8. Spoil tips and quarry inclines are some of the most dramatic monuments to be found in the central fells, many now the subject of a broad programme of conservation which plans to highlight the industrial heritage of the region. Beautiful to some and a blot on the landscape to others, some abandoned workings have been used for landfill. Others have been left open, particularly among the fells. One unintended consequence of this has been the creation of new ecological niches for rock and crag loving plants and for animals and birds, themselves the subject of conservation regulations.
9. A curious parallel can be found amongst those who collect artefacts today; a good storm will often be followed by a return to well-known exposures.
10. Evans, 1897: 117.
11. Bunch & Fell 1949; Clough 1973; Fell 1954; Houlder 1979; Plint 1962.
12. Grimes 1979; Evens *et al.* 1962; Fell 1964; Manby 1965; Stone & Wallis 1951.
13. Claris & Quartermaine 1989; Houlder 1979.
14. Clare Fell and Vin Davis have pointed out that on the basis of petrological identification, the central area of the fells contains materials that would be classed not only as Group VI but also Groups VIII, XI and XX (Fell and Davis 1988). There is even a measure of confusion and subjectivity in current attempts to characterise the limits of Group VI itself.
15. Hartley 1932; Oliver 1961. One translation of the Old Norse for Thunacar Knot, where Tim Clough excavated a Neolithic working floor, is 'the craggy hill of the thin man'.
16. Claris & Quartermaine 1989.
17. Griggs 1956.
18. Haszeldine & Haszeldine 2003.

CHAPTER 5

1. This became all the more marked in the early nineteenth century, when the focus for visits became yet more tightly drawn around the central Lakeland area.
2. Nicholson 1955.
3. The (urban) appetite for prints of the Lakes increased exponentially during the nineteenth century, as did the practice of naming new blocks of streets in the suburbs of expanding towns after notable Lakeland areas.
4. Though he wrote one of the most popular guides to the Lakes (1822), Wordsworth was also a jealous guardian of the area against tourists drawn from classes who, in his view, lacked the sensibilities to appreciate the scenery around them (Lowenthal 1991). Ruskin would later take the same view, despairing at the 'stupid herds of

modern tourists' that came in with the expansion of the rail network (Ruskin 1876). Access was apparently important to both, but only on their terms. Even at this early stage, there was a paradox – how to preserve an area both *for* and *from* the nation (Newby 1987).

5. A rather different line was taken by Harriet Martineau, who published her own guide to the Lakes in 1855. For her, the railways were important precisely because they offered the chance of escape from the town, not to mention an influx of much needed money and radical ideas.
6. Smith 1967.
7. Higham 1986.
8. Gelling 1984; Rollinson 1978; 1989; Whyte 1985; Winchester 1987.
9. Swainson Cowper 1891; Collingwood 1932; Quartermaine & Krupa 1994.
10. Armitt 1908; 1916. National Trust Historic Landscape Survey: Great Langdale. Winchester (1987) also suggests that farm names with the suffix '-place' are likely to be medieval in origin, reflecting the creation of what were often tenement farms in land designated as 'forest'.
11. The exhibition referred to in this interview was staged about ten years ago and since then, organisations like the Black Environmental Network have done a great deal to encourage minority ethnic communities to find their own way into the countryside. The situation is slowly changing, the National Parks and the National Trust establishing initiatives such as the Mosaic Project. That said, some of the few Asian and Afro-Caribbean walkers that I spoke to on the fells mentioned staring, silences in pubs and awkwardness, a sense that they were identified with the city and not with the country. Most were at least second or third generation British. Others pointed out the irony that their parents or grandparents had been born and raised in rural communities.
12. See Buntin 1993 for a rich and personal evocation of these themes.
13. This process was encouraged by a general contrast between the lowland area, where improvements and experiments in crop rotation by landowning gentry were already bearing fruit, and the higher dales where people often continued to rely upon grass. Punitive winters and a decline in the market for secondary products such as wool and linen weakened the resolve still further.
14. See Williamson 2002 for a broad and stimulating treatment of these changes.
15. The growth of tourism brought further changes. Old routes changed their purpose, if not their line, and new paths were established to carry visitors to specific places of scenic value such as Stickle Tarn or the Dungeon Ghyll waterfall. Hotels were also established, the farm at Middlefell Place seeing the building of the Old Dungeon Ghyll Hotel around the mid-nineteenth century, the New Dungeon Ghyll hotel later on. For many in the valley, tourism became part of the dual economy.
16. We may be imposing present on past when we assume that access was based on exclusive and sharply defined rights of ownership, especially when present connections are themselves remarkably varied. The same ground is identified with by the National Trust and the National Park, and by various hill-farming families. It is also a subject of close identification by climbers and fell walkers, a final resting place for ashes and an area for family and communal get-togethers. If you are talking with someone who has walked or climbed in the area for years, it isn't all that long before a sense of close identification emerges, often in response to 'newcomers'. Even now, there are many kinds of ownership which have no basis in title or deed.

17. Collingwood 1933. Our lack of knowledge about long cairns and related features in Cumbria is to some extent a function of the fact that the area has few of the more distinctive chambered tombs seen in other western regions. That and a lack of the systematic study mean that evidence for the character and chronology of sites is poor. Sometimes it is even difficult to determine whether sites are entirely constructed, or additions to prominent natural ridges or outcrops. More work would certainly help, though on this last point at least, we should allow that even natural outcrops and ridges may have been regarded as significant by communities at the time.
18. Kinnes & Longworth 1985; Masters, 1984.
19. Barnatt 1996; Thomas 1999; Tilley 1994.
20. The Neolithic use of caves and fissures for burial and for other forms of ritual is well attested in many parts of Britain. The nature of the conditions in these settings is often such that it suggests use for rituals of withdrawal and separation (Bradley 1999; Edmonds & Seaborne 2001; Thomas 1999).

CHAPTER 6

1. This is rather wishful thinking. For Ruskin, vision was essential for the proper appreciation of nature. In his essays on workers' education, he makes a great deal of how drawing is fundamental to the development of the correct gaze (Ruskin 1876). Reading between the lines, it is clear that touch, like manual labour, is quite literally of a lower order; even the senses broke along class divisions.
2. Walking as a poetic equivalent for the 'righteous' routine of rural life was part of the introverted experience of the Romantics. By Ruskin's time, it was a source of moral and physical improvement, laying the foundations for the 'outward bound' mentality that has shaped more recent interests and the management of the area.
3. The lobby for conservation was fired by quarrying and by the making of the Thirlmere reservoir in the 1870s and fostered by the 'Lake District Defence Society', formed in 1883 by Octavia Hill, Canon Rawnsley, Robert Hunter and John Ruskin. Their primary concern was protecting Wordsworth's 'national property' from the dual threats of unchecked industrial development and mass tourism. This became a yet more pressing concern in the decades after the First World War, when many aristocratic estates were broken up and offered for sale (Cannadine 1992). By then, when conservation was becoming an important political issue, concern was met locally by organisations such as the 'Friends of the Lake District', formed in 1934 by such luminaries as the historian George Trevellyan, who gave a good deal of land, including parts of the Langdales, to the National Trust.
4. The lobby was both massive and varied, arguments taking different paths, often as a function of class. Encouraged by organisations such as the Youth Hostelling Association, thousands of ramblers poured into the Lake District and by the early twentieth century, it was not uncommon for excursions to contain more than a hundred, sometimes several hundred, people (Taylor 1997). Some of these campaigned for access along established routes, footpaths and other tracks where common use maintained customary rights of way. Others took a harder line, more radical rambling and climbing groups such as the Manchester Ramblers Federation and Red Rope, who were politically committed to more basic principles of open access (Darby 2000; Lowe 1989; Newby 1987). For some at least, the lobby that would eventually lead to the formation of National Parks at the end of the 1940s dealt with

The Langdales

only part of the problem. It opened things up to some degree, but it still left many older interests and authorities intact (See the excellent *Landscape and Englishness* by David Matless 1998).

5. For a book that manages to convey the changing character and context of climbing and something of the experience, see *Native Stones* by David Craig (Craig 1987).
6. '. . . *Shall we suppose it is a greater pleasure to the sportsman to pursue a trivial animal, than it is to the man of taste to pursue the beauties of nature: to follow her through all her recesses? to obtain a sudden glance, as she flits past him in some airy shape? to trace her through the mazes of the cover . . .* ' (Gilpin 1792). From an early stage, perspectives on the fells have often been heavily gendered; the accounts of early mountaineers are also full of references to virgin peaks, coy slopes, curves, assaults and conquests (Darby 2000). How far things have changed since then depends on who you talk to. Even a brief glance at the names of many climbing routes reveals a continuing predilection for directed sexual imagery.

CHAPTER 7

1. Barbara Hepworth, in the catalogue for *Retrospective Exhibition 1927-1954*, Whitechapel Art Gallery, London.
2. Clough & Cummins 1988.
3. Darbishire 1873.
4. Bradley & Edmonds 1993.
5. The term 'club' was initially used in the mid-nineteenth century to identify larger blades with a distinct waisting towards the butt. On analogy with the wooden exercise clubs that people used in callisthenics or with implements like the *Maori Mere*, it was assumed that these were hand held. By the end of the century, this had been largely rejected, though the term has stuck (Evans 1897). Since then, the classification of blades has conventionally distinguished between 'Cumbrian' axes and 'variants', the latter often seen as a result of the working down of larger forms (Bradley & Edmonds 1993; Fell 1964; Manby 1979). This may be so in some cases and there are certainly examples where side facets have clearly been truncated by further flaking and grinding. That said, it is likely that there were many blades that from the outset lacked the distinctive side facets and other features associated with the 'Cumbrian' form (see Cooney & Mandal 1998 for more detailed discussion of this point).
6. Henry Moore in *Henry Moore on sculpture*, London, Macdonald 1966. The 'truth to material' advocated by Moore and others was a reaction specific to its time, and one to which he did not always adhere. But when he talked of the relationship with material that direct carving required, he recognised a quality to the act of working that, whatever it meant, was probably no less important in the Neolithic.

CHAPTER 8

1. Clough & Cummins 1979.
2. See Thomas 1999 and Whittle 2003 for recent discussions of identity in the Neolithic.
3. Weiner 1985.
4. Bradley 1984; Bradley & Edmonds 1993.
5. Hutchinson 1776; Stukeley 1776. Such ruined architectures were an important element in Gilpin's vision of the Picturesque, and the legacy of that view would remain to influence the Romantics and even Ruskin's attitude to the conservation of medieval buildings.

6. Soffe & Clare 1988.
7. Horne, Macleod & Oswald 2001.
8. Oswald, Dyer & Barber 2001.
9. Burl 1976.
10. Collingwood 1933: 176.
11. Stories are attached to many circles and henges. In 1610, Camden recorded a 'folktale' that the stones within the henge at Mayburgh had been robbed during the building of Penrith Castle. In the later eighteenth century, William Stukeley talked of the 'British wrestling place calld King Arthurs round table' and many circles have associations with dancing, with witches and the Devil. For example, the circle at Swinside has an older name 'Sunken Kirk' – a reference to a local story that the building of a church was thwarted by the Devil, who came each night and drew the masonry down into the earth. This is by no means uncommon and the prominence of many sites in oral tradition suggests a continued importance in the local imagination: as meeting places, as sites to be respected and sometimes even feared, the latter a response often encouraged by the Church.
12. Only one standing stone survives in the interior of Mayburgh, but early accounts suggest that there were originally more. Used by John Aubrey, William Dugdale's unpublished description of 1664 suggests an arrangement of four tall stones at the centre of the monument with additional stones flanking the entrance. Ploughing had already taken place in the interior by the time that William Stukeley recorded the site in 1725, but the stones seen by Dugdale were still there, and he comments upon the destruction or removal of others 'a year or two ago' (Dymond 1891; Topping 1992).

CHAPTER 9
1. The Fall. *Contraflow*.

BIBLIOGRAPHY

Adams, J. 1988: *Mines of the Lake District Fells*. Clapham. Dalesman.
Adkins, R. & Jackson, R. 1978: *Neolithic axes from the River Thames*. London. British Museum Occasional Paper 1.
Armitt, M. 1908: 'Fullers and freeholders of the Parish of Grasmere'. *Transactions of the Cumberland and Westmorland Archaeological Society* 8:136-205.
Armitt, M. 1916: *Rydal*. Kendal. Titus Wilson.

Barnatt, J. 1989: *Stone circles of Britain*. Oxford. British Archaeological Reports 215.
Barnatt, J. 1996: 'Moving between the monuments: Paths and people in the Neolithic landscapes of the Peak District'. *Northern Archaeology* 13/14: 45-62.
Barnes, F. 1963: 'Discovery of four roughed-out stone axes at Skelmore Heads, July 1959'. *Transactions of the Cumberland and Westmorland Archaeological Society* 63:27-30.
Barrell, J. 1980: *The dark side of the landscape*. Cambridge. Cambridge University Press.
Barrett, J.C. 1994: *Fragments from antiquity*. Oxford. Blackwells.
Beckensall, S. 2002: *Prehistoric Rock Art in Cumbria – Landscape and monuments*. Stroud. Tempus.
Berger, J. 1973: 'Ways of seeing'. London. BBC.
Bonsall, C., Sutherland, D., Tipping, R. & Cherry, J. 1989: 'The Eskmeals project:late Mesolithic settlement and economy in north-west England'. In Bonsall, C. (ed.) *The Mesolithic in Europe*. Edinburgh. John Donald.
Boon, G.C. 1976: 'An early Tudor coiner's mould and the workings of Borrowdale graphite'. *Transactions of the Cumberland and Westmorland Archaeological Society* 76: 97-132.
Bradley, R. 1984: *The social foundations of prehistoric Britain*. London. Longmans.
Bradley, R. 1990: *The passage of arms*. Cambridge. Cambridge University Press.
Bradley, R. 1998: *The significance of monuments*. London. Routledge.
Bradley, R. 2000: *The archaeology of natural Places*. London. Routledge.

Bradley, R. & Edmonds, M. 1993: *Interpreting the axe trade*. Cambridge. Cambridge University Press.

Bridge, D. 1992: '"Wad" in Cumbria'. In *Beneath the Lakeland Fells*. Cumbria Amenity Trust Mining History 43-54. Ulverston. Red Earth.

Briggs, S. 1976: 'Notes on the distribution of some raw materials in later Prehistoric Britain'. In Burgess, C. & Miket, R. (eds) *Settlement and economy in the third and second millennia BC*. 267-282. Oxford. British Archaeological Reports 33.

Briggs, S. 1989: 'Axe-making traditions in Cumbrian stone'. *Archaeological Journal* 146: 101-112.

Bunch, B. & Fell, C. 1949: 'A stone axe factory at Pike of Stickle, Great Langdale, Westmorland'. *Proceedings of the Prehistoric Society* 15: 1-20.

Bunce, M. 1994: *The countryside ideal: Anglo-American images of landscape*. London. Routledge.

Buntin, T.F. 1993: *Life in Langdale: The memoirs of a Lakeland farmer*. Kendal. Titus Wilson.

Burke, E. 1757: *Philosophical enquiry into the origin of our ideas of the Sublime and the Beautiful*. Oxford. Oxford University Press.

Burl, A. 1976: *Stone Circles of the British Isles*. Yale. Yale University Press.

Burl, A. 1988: 'Without sharp north: Alexander Thom and the Great Stone Circles of Cumbria'. In Ruggles, C. (ed.) *Records in Stone*. 175-205. Cambridge. Cambridge University Press.

Cherry, J. & Cherry, P. 1983: 'Prehistoric habitation sites in West Cumbria: Part 1'. *Transactions of the Cumberland and Westmorland Archaeological Society* 83, 1-14.

Cherry, J. & Cherry, P. 1984: 'Prehistoric habitation sites in West Cumbria: Part 2'. *Transactions of the Cumberland and Westmorland Archaeological Society* 84, 1-17.

Cherry, J. & Cherry, P. 1985: 'Prehistoric habitation sites in West Cumbria: Part 3'. *Transactions of the Cumberland and Westmorland Archaeological Society* 85, 1-10.

Cherry, J. & Cherry, P. 1986: 'Prehistoric habitation sites in West Cumbria: Part 4'. *Transactions of the Cumberland and Westmorland Archaeological Society* 86, 1-17.

Cherry, J. & Cherry, P. 1987a: 'Prehistoric habitation sites in West Cumbria: Part 5'. *Transactions of the Cumberland and Westmorland Archaeological Society* 87, 1-10.

Cherry, J. & Cherry, P. 1987b: *Prehistoric habitation sites on the Limestone uplands of eastern Cumbria*. Kendal. Cumberland and Westmorland Archaeological Society Research Volume 2.

Claris, P. & Quartermaine, J. 1989: 'The Neolithic quarries and axe factory sites of Great Langdale and Scafell Pike: a new field survey'. *Proceedings of the Prehistoric Society* 55: 1-25.

Clark, J.D.G. 1965: 'Traffic in stone axe and adze blades'. *Economic History Review* (2nd series) 18: 1-28.

Clough, T. 1973: 'Excavations on a Langdale chipping site in 1969 and 1970'. *Transactions of the Cumberland and Westmorland Archaeological Society* 73: 25-46.

Clough, T. & Cummins, W.A. (eds) 1979: *Stone axe studies*. London. Council for British Archaeology Research Report 23.

Clough, T. & Cummins, W.A. (eds) 1988: *Stone axe studies 2*. London. Council for British Archaeology Research Report 67.

Collingwood, R.G. 1933: 'An introduction to the prehistory of Cumberland, Westmorland and Lancashire north of the sands'. *Transactions of the Cumberland and Westmorland Archaeological Society* 33:163-200.

Collingwood, R.G. 1946: *The idea of history*. Oxford. Oxford University Press.

Collingwood, W.G. 1932: *The Lake Counties*. London.
Cooney, G. 2000: *Neolithic landscapes of Ireland*. London. Routledge.
Cooney, G. & Mandal, S. 1998: *The Irish Stone Axe Project*. Co. Wicklow. Wordwell.
Cosgrove, D. 1984: *Social formation and symbolic landscape*. London.

Daniels, S. 1988: 'The political iconography of woodland in later Georgian England'. In Cosgrove, D. & Daniels, S. (eds) *The Iconography of Landscape*. Cambridge. Cambridge University Press 43-82.
Darbishire, R. 1873: 'Notes on discoveries at Ehenside Tarn, Cumberland'. *Archaeologia* 44: 273-292.
Darby, W.J. 2000: *Landscape and Identity*. Oxford. Berg.
Darvill, T. & Thomas, J. (eds) 1996: *Neolithic houses in northwest Europe and beyond*. Oxbow Monograph 57. Oxford. Oxbow.
Dymond, C.W. 1891: 'Mayburgh and King Arthur's Round Table'. *Transactions of the Cumberland and Westmorland Archaeological Society* (1) 11:187-219.

Edmonds, M. 1995: *Stone tools and society*. London. Batsford.
Edmonds, M. 1999: *Ancestral geographies of the Neolithic. Landscape monuments and memory*. London. Routledge.
Edmonds, M. & Seaborne, T. 2001: *Prehistory in the Peak*. Stroud. Tempus.
Evans, J. 1897: *Ancient stone Implements of Great Britain*. London. Longmans.
Evelyn, J. 1664: *Silva, or a discourse of Forest-Trees*.
Evens, E., Smith, I. & Wallis, F. 1962: 'Fourth report of the sub-committee of the South Western federation of Museums and Art Galleries on the petrological identification of stone axes. *Proceedings of the Prehistoric Society* 28: 209-266.

Fell, C. 1950: 'The Great Langdale stone axe factory'. *Transactions of the Cumberland and Westmorland Archaeological Society* 50:1-13.
Fell, C. 1954: 'Further notes on the Great Langdale axe factory'. *Proceedings of the Prehistoric Society* 20:238-239.
Fell, C. 1964: 'The Cumbrian type of polished stone axe and its distribution in Britain'. *Proceedings of the Prehistoric Society* 30: 39-55.
Fell, C. & Davis, R.V. 1988: 'The petrological identification of stone implements from Cumbria'. In Clough, T. & Cummins, W.A. (eds) *Stone axe studies 2*. London. Council for British Archaeology Research Report 67. 71-77.

Gelling, M. 1984: *Place names in the landscape*. London. John Dent.
Gilpin, W. 1786: *Observations relative chiefly to picturesque beauty, made in the year 1772, on several parts of England; especially the mountains and lakes*. London.
Gosden, C. 1999: *Archaeology and Anthropology: A changing relationship*. London. Routledge.
Grimes, W.F. 1979: 'The history of implement petrology in Britain'. In Clough, T. & Cummins, W.A. (eds) *Stone axe studies*. London. Council for British Archaeology Research Report 23. 1-4.

Harding, A. & Young, R. 1979: 'Reconstruction of the hafting methods and function of stone implements'. In Clough, T. & Cummins, W.A. (eds) 1979: *Stone axe studies*. London. Council for British Archaeology Research Report 23.102-15.

Hartley, J.J. 1932: 'The volcanic and other igneous rocks of Great and Little Langdale, Westmorland'. *Proceedings of the Geological Association* 43: 32-69.

Haszeldine, R. & Haszeldine, R. 2003: 'Neolithic, natural or new? Critical observations of cup and ring petroglyphs in Langdale, Cumbria'. *Transactions of the Cumberland and Westmorland Archaeological Society* (3) 3: 1-23.

Higham, N. 1986: *The northern counties to AD 1000*. Harlow. Longman.

Horne, P.D., Maclod, D. & Oswald, A. 2001: 'A probable Neolithic causewayed enclosure in northern England'. *Antiquity* 75: 17-18.

Houlder, C. 1979: 'The Langdale and Scafell Pike axe factory sites: a field survey'. In Clough, T. & Cummins, W.A. (eds) *Stone axe studies*. London. Council for British Archaeology Research Report 23. 87-89.

Hutchinson, W. 1776: *An excursion to the lakes in Westmorland and Cumberland; with a tour through part of the northern counties in the years 1773 and 1774*. London. Wilkie and Charnley.

Johnson, S. 1988: 'Iron mining on the high fells above Eskdale and Langdale, and miners' roads'. *Transactions of the Cumberland and Westmorland Archaeological Society* 88: 246-248.

Kendrick, T. 1925: *The Axe Age: A study in British Prehistory*. London. Methuen.

Kinnes, I. & Longworth, I. 1985: *Catalogue of the excavated Prehistoric and Romano-British material in the Greenwell Collection*. London. British Museum.

Knowles, W.J. 1906: 'Stone axe factories near Cushendall'. *Journal of the Royal Society of Antiquaries of Ireland* 16: 383-394.

Lowenthal, D. 1991: 'British national identity and the English landscape'. *Rural History* 2 (2): 205-230.

Manby, T. 1965: 'The distribution of roughout, Cumbrian and related axes of Lake District origin in northern England'. *Transactions of the Cumberland and Westmorland Archaeological Society* 65:1-37.

Manby, T. 1979: 'Typology, material and distribution of flint and stone axes in Yorkshire'. In Clough, T. & Cummins, W. A. (eds) *Stone axe studies*. London. Council for British Archaeology Research Report 23. 65-81.

Marshall, J.D. & Davies-Shiel, M. 1977: *The industrial archaeology of the Lake counties*. Beckermet. Michael Moon.

Martineau, H. 1855: *Complete Guide to the English Lakes*. London. Whittaker & Co.

Masters, L. 1984: 'The Neolithic long cairns of Cumbria and Northumberland'. In Miket, R. & Burgess, C. (eds) *Between and Beyond the walls*. Edinburgh. John Donald. 52-73.

Matless, D. 1998: *Landscape and Englishness*. London. Reaktion.

Mcintyre, J. 1937: 'Four polished stone axes'. *Transactions of the Cumberland and Westmorland Archaeological Society* 37: 152-154.

Moore, H. 1966: *Henry Moore on Sculpture*. London. Macdonald.

Newby, H. 1987: *Country life: A social history of rural England*. London. Weidenfield & Nicholson.

Newman, G. 1987: *The rise of English Nationalism: A cultural history 1740-1830*. New York. St Martin's Press.

Nicholson, N. 1955: *The Lakers: The adventures of the first tourists*. London. Robert Hale.
Nicholson, N. 1963: *Portrait of the Lakes*. London. Robert Hale.

Oliver, R.L. 1961: 'The Borrowdale volcanic and associated rocks of the Scafell area, Lake District'. *Journal of the Geological Society* 117: 377-417.
Oswald, A. Dyer, C. & Barber, M. 2000: *The Creation of monuments. Neolithic Causewayed Enclosures in the British Isles*. London. English Heritage.

Pennington, W. 1970: 'Vegetational history in the north-west of England – a regional study'. In Walker, D. & West, R.G. (eds) *Studies in the vegetational history of the British Isles* 41: 41-80. Cambridge. Cambridge University Press.
Pennington, W. 1975: 'The effect of man on the environments of north-west England: the use of absolute pollen diagrams'. In Evans, J.G., Limbrey, S. & Cleere, H. (eds) *The effect of man on the landscape: The highland zone*. London. Council for British Archaeology Research Report 11: 74-86.
Phillips, A.P. 1979: Stone axes in ethnographic situatons: some examples from New Guinea and the Solomon Islands. In Clough, T. & Cummins, W.A. (eds) *Stone axe studies*. London. Council for British Archaeology Research Report 23: 108-112.
Phythian-Adams, C. 1991: Local History and National History: The quest for the peoples of England. *Rural History* (2) 1: 1-23.
Pitts, M. 1996: The stone axe in Neolithic Britain. *Proceedings of the Prehistoric Society* 62: 311-372.
Plint, R.G. 1962: 'Stone axe factory sites in the Cumbrian fells'. *Transactions of the Cumberland and Westmorland Archaeological Society* 62: 1-26.
Pollard, J. 1999: 'These places have their moments. Occupation practices in the British Neolithic'. In Bruck, J. & Goodman, M. *Making places in the prehistoric world: themes in settlement archaeology*. London. Longmans.
Postlethwaite, J. 1913: *Mines and mining in the English Lake District*. Whitehaven. Michael Moon.
Price, U. 1810: *Essays on the Picturesque* Vol. 1. London.
Pryor, F. 1998: *Etton: Excavations at a Neolithic causewayed enclosure*. English Heritage Research Report 18. London. English Heritage.

Quartermaine, J. & Krupa, M. 1994: *Thingmount, Little Langdale, Cumbria: An Archaeological survey*. Lancaster University Archaeological Unit. Lancaster.

Rackham, O. 1990: *Trees and Woodland in the British landscape*. London. J.M. Dent.
Rawnsley, H.D. 1902: 'Stone implements lately found at Portinscale, near Derwentwater'. *Proceedings of the Society of Antiquaries*. 2nd series 19: 37-40.
Robinson, T. 1709: *An essay towards the natural history of Westmorland and Cumberland*. London. Freeman.
Rollinson, W. 1978: *Life and tradition in the Lake District*. London. John Dent.
Rollinson, W. 1989: *The Lake District landscape heritage*. Newton Abbot. David & Charles.
Ruskin, J. 1876: *A protest against the extension of the railways in the Lake District*. Windermere. Somervell.

Schama, S. 1996: *Landscape and Memory*. New York. Alfred Knopf.

Shee Twohig, E. 1981: *The Megalithic Art of Western Europe*. Oxford. Clarendon Press.

Soffe, G. & Clare, T. 1988: 'New evidence of ritual monuments at Long Meg and her Daughters, Cumbria'. *Antiquity* 62:552-7.

Stone, J.F.S. & Wallis, F.S. 1951: 'Third report of the sub-committee of the South-Western federation of Museums and Art Galleries on the petrological identification of stone axes'. *Proceedings of the Prehistoric Society* 17: 99-158.

Stukeley, W. 1776: *Itinerarium Curiosum*. London. Baker & Leigh.

Swainson Cowper, H. 1891: 'Law Ting at Fell Foot, Little Langdale, Westmorland'. *Transactions of the Cumberland and Westmorland Archaeological Society* 11: 1-5.

Thomas, N. 1991: *Entangled objects*. Harvard. Harvard University Press.

Thomas, J. 1999: *Understanding the Neolithic*. London. Routledge.

Thomas, J. & Tilley, C. 1993: 'The axe and the torso'. In Tilley, C. (ed.) *Interpretive archaeology*. Oxford. Berg.

Tilley, C. 1994: *A phenomenology of landscape*. Oxford. Berg.

Topping, P. 1998: *Neolithic landscapes*. Oxford. Oxbow monograph.

Tyler, I. 1994: *Honister Slate*. Caldbeck. Blur Rock.

Tyler, I. 1995: *Seathwaite Wad*. Carlisle. Blue Rock.

Walker, D. 1965: 'The post-glacial period in the Langdale Fells, English Lake District'. *New Phytologist* 64: 488-510.

Walker, D. 2001: 'The dates of human impacts on the environment at Ehenside Tarn, Cumbria'. *Transactions of the Cumberland and Westmorland Archaeological Society* (3) 1: 1-20.

Waterhouse, J. 1985: *The stone circles of Cumbria*. Southampton. Camelot Press.

Weiner, A. 1985: 'Inalienable wealth'. *American Ethnologist* 12.2: 210-227.

West, T. 1778: *A guide to the Lakes: Dedicated to the lovers of landscape studies and to all who have visited, or intend to visit the Lakes in Cumberland, Westmorland and Lancashire*. London & Kendal.

Whittle, A.W.R. 1996: *The creation of new worlds*. Cambridge. Cambridge University Press.

Whittle, A.W.R. 1998: 'Moving on and moving around'. In Topping, P. (ed.) *Neolithic landscapes*. Oxford. Oxbow.

Whittle, A.W.R. 2003: *Dimensions of Neolithic Life*. London. Routledge.

Whyte, I. 1985: 'Shielings and the upland pastoral economy of the Lake District in Medieval and Early Modern times'. In Baldwin, J. & Whyte, I. (eds) *The Scandinavians in Cumbria*. Edinburgh. Scottish Society for Northern Studies. 103-117.

Williams, R. 1973: *The country and the city*. London. Penguin.

Williamson, T. 2002: *The transformation of Rural England*. Edinburgh. Windgather Press.

Winchester, A.J.L. 1987: *Landscape and society in Medieval Cumbria*. Edinburgh. John Donald.

Wordsworth, W. 1822: *A guide through the district of the lakes in the north of England with a description of the scenery etc. For the use of tourists and residents*. Kendal. Hudson & Nicholson.

INDEX

Ambleside 100, 153
Appleby horse fair 168
Ash Busk 113
Aughertree Fell 176

Bacabeck 113
Bank 74
Barony of Kendale 104
Baysbrown 100, 105
Belmont 38
Big Bitts 113
Birkett, J. 130
Black Combe 21, 23
Black Environmental Network 210
Blea Tarn 61
Bonfire Cave 121
Borderstone 111
Borrowdale Volcanics 67, 69, 115
Bowfell 73, 81
Bradley, Richard 207
Brantwood 61, 204
Brats Hill 187
Briggs, Stephen 207
Broad stand 84
Browney Gill 73
Burke, Edmund 13

Cabinets of Curiosities 35
Carrock Fell 176

Castle How 104
Castle Howe 102
Castlerigg 15, 176, 178, 179, 180, 181, 182
Celts 34
Chapel Stile 72, 74, 111
Cistercians 54
Claife Station 203
Clare, John 18
Claude glasses 13, 97, 203
Coleridge, Samuel 16, 84, 88
Colt Howe 74
Collingwood, R.G. 21, 22, 23, 24, 179
Company of Mines Royal 69
Conishead Priory 104
Coniston 69, 204
Coniston Old Man 88
Coppicing 51, 59
Copt Howe 92
Cowshot Howe 111
Craig Lwyd 40, 194
Crosby Garrett 121
Culture History 22
Cumbrian Clubs 164, 166

Dalehead 69
Dalton, John 70
Darbishire, R.D. 27
Darby 203

The Langdales

Davis, Vin 209
Dixon, Anthony 111
Doctor syntax 204
Dog Hole Cave 121
Drigg 58, 115
Duddon 52
Dungeon Ghyll 140, 210

Eden Valley 58, 77, 79, 120, 121, 153
Ehenside Tarn 27, 29, 30, 42, 157, 158
Ellers 111
Elterwater 52, 74
Elva Plain 180
Eskdale 50, 115
Esh Hause 67
Eskmeals 58
Esthwaite 50
Etton 195
Evans, Sir John 36, 80

Fell, Clare 80, 206, 209
Fell and Rock Climbing Club 130
Fell Foot Farm 102
Forestry Commission 50
Forest silver 53
Furness 115, 153
Furness Abbey 52

Gala Field 113
Gift exchange 173
Gilpin, William 13, 207
Glaramara 81, 139, 166
Gosden, Chris 203
Grasmere 108, 111, 112
Graves, Robert 128
Gray, Thomas 16, 70
Great End 81
Great Gable 130
Grey Croft 179, 180, 185
Grizedale 54

Hackett Forge 73
Haddenham 195
Hafting 158, 159, 160
Hardknott 100, 196
Harrison Pike 11, 133, 139
Harry Place 11, 52, 92, 105

Hawkshead 108, 112
Heathwaite 120
Helvellyn 67
Herdwick Sheep 100, 139
Honister 69
Howe Robin 176
Huntingstile 111

Ireland 25, 79, 166, 176
Irish Sea 25
Irton 120
Isle of Man 79, 166, 176

Jack's Rake 130

Keeping while giving 173
Kemp Howe 180
Kendal 108
Kenworthy, Revd J.W. 27
Keswick 153
King Arthur's Round Table 177, 179, 181, 182
Kirkhead Cave 121
Knowles, William 39

Lacra 181
Lake District Defence Society 211
Langdale Combe 57, 61, 102
Langstrath 73
Lingmell Ghyll 133
Lingmoor 74
Loft Crag 11, 82
Long Meg and her Daughters 176, 180, 182

Manchester Ramblers Federation 211
Martineau, Harriet 210
Mayburgh 177, 179, 185, 213
Mickleden Valley 83, 100, 192
Middlefell Place 105
Millbeck 52, 108
Mossthorn 120
Mount's Bay 40
Murray, W.H. 128

Nape's Needle 130
National Trust 48, 206, 211

Index

Newlands 69
Nicholson, Norman 7, 67
Nick Stick Seat 106, 108
Nummer, Billy 39

Oak Howe farm 111
Oak How Needle 113
Ore Gap 73

Pavey Ark 100
Pike of Stickle 11, 83, 196
Pillar 129, 130
Pitt Rivers, Augustus 38
Polissoir 157
Pollarding 47
Portinscale 38
Potter, Beatrix 20
Pye Howe 111

Raiset Pike 120
Ravenglass 24
Raw Head 57
Raw Pike 57, 104, 113
Red Rope 209
Red Tarn 73
Rheged 21
Ring Garth 105, 107, 108, 113
Robinson Place 73, 105, 108
Rossett 100, 105
Ruskin, John 7, 15, 61, 88, 97, 127, 128, 204

St Bees 24, 58
Sampson's Bratful 120
Scafell Pike 81, 82, 133, 139, 140, 166
Scale Ghyll 57, 100, 102
Scott, Sir Walter 35
Seathwaite 70, 206
Seathwaite Fell Tuffs 81
Seatoller Fell 69
Sellafield 27, 192
Shap 181
Shoe last axes 34
Sidehouse 105
Side Pike 114
Simpson, Edward 39
Skelmore Heads 39, 120, 176

Skelwith Bridge 74
Skelwith Force 11, 15
Skiddaw Slate 67, 69
Solway Moss 42
Solway Plain 153, 172
Sour Milk Ghyll 70
Smith, William 39
Sprinkling Tarn 81
Stake Beck 133
Stake Pass 114
Stake Pass Industry 80
Statesmen 112, 113
Stickle Ghyll 108
Stickle Tarn 52, 81, 100, 102, 133, 210
Stockdale Moor 120
Stool End 105, 108
Swinside 179, 180, 187

Thingmount 102
Thorn Crag 133, 140
Thrang Crag 74
Thunacarr Knott 133
Tievebulliagh 39, 40, 79
Trainford Brow 120
Troughton Beck 57

Wad (graphite) 69, 70
Wall End 108, 114
Walthwaite 111
Walney Island 58
West, Thomas 11, 49, 99, 203
Wet Parrock 113
Whittle, Alasdair 205
Wigton 38
Williamson's Moss 24
Windermere 15
Wood Hinning 113
Wordsworth, William 13, 16, 18, 19, 67, 97, 113, 115, 180
Workers Sports Federation 130
Wormal Crag 57
Wrynose Gill 73

Yew Crags 69

223

If you are interested in purchasing
other books published by Tempus, or in case you have
difficulty finding any Tempus books in your local bookshop,
you can also place orders directly through our website

www.tempus-publishing.com